Reviews for True

For as long as I known Miles McKee, I have been regaled with yarns about Willie Murphy and fantastical goings on in Maghera. Through the richness of Miles' story telling, this colourful character formed in my minds eye and I knew instantly the moment I encountered him - not the actual Willie Murphy, or the dozens of other characters in this book - but every town and village in Ireland has a Willie and I've met et least one!

Thanks to Miles' for amassing this wonderful compendium of characters and their antics. It should be categorised under Education and used extensively as a primer for anyone wishing to understand Ireland and its people.

Stephen McIlwrath, Managing Director, Avalon Guitars.

Every success to Miles with these True Tales. I'm sure they'll travel the length of Main Street, turn left for the Glen and onwards, to rise above the Sperrins and well beyond, delighting both those at home, and the South Derry diaspora.

Every good wish.

Eleanor Methven. Actress.

You will 'roll with laughter' as you journey back in time to a less sophisticated era and meet just some of the many characters, who didn't suffer from insanity, but enjoyed every minute of it, and who lived in and around the 'wee' town of Maghera , which nestles at the bottom of the Glenshane Pass, County Derry/Londonderry N.Ireland. This book of short tales, captured for posterity, and told by Miles McKee in his own witty and inimitable style will certainly lift the spirits and give an insight into the humorous and carefree side of life in rural Ireland!Great as a holiday read! Or simply for a night 'by the fire'.But if you don't enjoy a laugh .... this book is not for you!

John Burns
Former High Sheriff of County Derry/Londonderry

TRUE TALES OF MAGHERA AND BEYOND

For the benefit of those who are not native to the Maghera district, I first have to say that the name of our wee town is pronounced, "Mah-hurrah." I say this because one of my American friends once looked at our village on a map and thought I hailed from "Maag-ha-Gra." Maag-ha-gra! … Sounds like a Mohican war chant! .

Many of the following yarns feature a gentleman named Willie Murphy. He and his wife Bella were, as they say, 'fond of the drink'. Like R.L Marshall's character, 'Guldy', they lived in a world, "in which whiskey occupied an undisputed place at the top of the scale and 'blow-hard' near the bottom, with a roughly graduated list of liquids of differing alcoholic content in between."

I grew up listening to tales of Willie and Bella and others. Many of them are true. Doubtless a few are may be invented … but why let the truth get in the way of a good yarn? Willie was renowned for his sharp wit and turn of phrase. Some stories about him have even made it into the repertoires of stand up comics like the one where he went to see Dr. Love and complained about not feeling well. After a thorough examination, Dr. Love said he could find nothing wrong. "It must just be the drink," says Dr Love. To which Willie replied, "Alright then Doctor, I'll come back when you're sober."

Maghera was rich with characters. But we were not alone. As I have travelled, I have been privileged to also hear yarns in various parts of Ireland. It seems that almost every town has had its own set of characters. I only wish all their stories had been collected.

It is important to stress, at this point, that this is not a collection of jokes, but rather a compilation of yarns --- and there is a difference. The joke is a concocted story designed to deliver a good punch line while a yarn, though a good source of entertainment, is usually an amusing story based on actual events.

The characters in this book did exist. They lived and breathed in Maghera, County Derry/Londonderry and in other parts of Ireland in days long gone. They both said and did things that earned them the well deserved designation of 'characters'.

Here's to Peter Duffy, a wee man who never missed going to a wake, for that would have meant that he would have missed a cup of tea. Here's to The Flying Barber (the Fairy Campbell) who, when he tried to sell you a watch, would say, "It's a good one and I couldn't tell a lie for I'm only coming from the Altar Railings." Here's to Peacock O'Neill, The Gomey, Mrs Cassidy, 'Redd the Road' Riley, Carnegie Cleek, Jimmy the Spit, Mark Murray the dancing policeman, Mary Ann McGirr, the breaker of windows, the March Hare, Paddy Buckley and them all.

Thanks

My thanks go to all who have told or provided me with yarns through the years, especially Freddy Joe Tohill, Charles McGuigan, Jacqueline Conway, John Marquess and Stephen Richardson of Maghera. Also, thanks go to Nick Cashin of New Ross County Wexford and to my sister Hilary (McKee) McCarthy of Omagh.

Again, thanks goes to my cousins, Dr. Richard Burns of Coleraine, Rosalind Gillespie of Portrush and Cynthia Chamberlin of Switzerland. Thanks also to the present day Maghera Burns clan, John, Alan, George, Shaun and Gary.

Major thanks also go to members of my Maghera family, the late Joseph Burns MP, the late Col. John F Burns, the late Dr. William Burns, the late Dr. George Burns, the late R.E. Burns, and my parents, the late Edna (Burns) McKee and C. G McKee.

Special thanks goes to my good and dear friend James Buckley, 'Auld Buck' of Ballyhighland, County Wexford. Extra special thanks goes to my editor and beautiful wife Gillian McKee.

Here then are a few yarns about Murphy and other assorted characters from Maghera and regions beyond.

WILLIE MURPHY AND OTHER ASSORTED CHARACTERS

The Tourists

Tourists used to be a common sight in Maghera. They were often good for a story. Take this one for example.

Willie Murphy was standing at the Hall Street corner when a car pulls up and a man sticks his head out the window and asks, "Will this road take me to Tobermore?"

"I don't know," says Murphy, "I've been standing here for half an hour and it hasn't taken me anywhere yet."

Another American tourist stopped Willie Murphy on Hall Street one day and asked, "Tell me buddy, were there any great men born in this village?"

Hall Street, Maghera, from Quinn's Corner

Murphy replied, "No sir, only babies."

On yet another occasion a Canadian visitor engaged him in conversation and asked, "Have you lived here all your life?"

Murphy quietly smiled and replied, "Not yet."

The O'Murphy Clan

On yet another occasion Murphy had 'fallen in' with an American tourist in O'Hara's Bar. They were getting on famously and the American says, "Tell me this Buddy. I thought that all Irish last names began with an 'O'. You've got O'Hara, O'Neill, O'Casey, O'Donnell, O'Leary but your name is just plain and simple Murphy. Surely it should be O'Murphy?"

"Well to be quite honest with you," says Willie, "there's something in what you say for there's no family in the country more worthy of the name O'Murphy than us."

"And why's that?" inquired the American.

"Because we owe everyone," says Willie.

Speaking In Tongues

Willie Murphy and Stick Leg McMurray were standing in the Bank Square one day when a tourist came up and said, "Parlez vous francais?" They shook their heads

"Sprechen sie Deutch?"

"No."

"Habla Español?"

Again their reply was in the negative.

"Parla L'Italiano?"

Yet again they shook their heads.

The gentleman walked off and Stick Leg says "Willie do you not think we'd be better employed taking night classes to learn a few foreign languages."

"Ach not at all" says Murphy, "Sure that poor auld crater knows four and look all the far it got him."

Auld McGaughy

'Auld McGaughy' was drinking in McMaster's pub and he says to the man sitting down at the end of the bar, "I should know you shouldn't I, for I've seen you often enough?"

"Aye deed you do know me," says the man, "My name's Flynn and I live the other side of Gulladuff" "Ach I remember you now," says Auld McGaughy, "there were two of you, two brothers, one of you died in a fire and the other lived. Which one are you?"

Pity For Pat McKenna

One day Willie Murphy stopped to talk to Stick Leg McMurray outside Noone's grocery shop. "Harry," says he, "did you hear that Father Duffy refused to bury Pat McKenna in the graveyard?"

Stick Leg's face took on a look of disgusted shock.

"My God!," he said, "Why in the name of thunder did he do that?"

"He wasn't dead," says Murphy.

Mickey And Stick Leg

Mickey Shoddy was a small cross-eyed man. One day he and Stick Leg McMurray accidentally collided on the footpath outside Harry Crawford's.

"Why don't you look where you're going," roared Mickey.

"I will in future," shouted Stick Leg, "but in the meantime why don't you go where you're looking."

The New Shoes

Jimmy Kelly had ordered up a new pair of shoes from Bob Picken, one of the local cobblers. When he finally tried them on he looked at Mr. Picken and said, "Well they fit all right Mr. Picken, but will they keep my feet dry?" Bob Picken looked at him and said, "Well Jimmy, it's like this, if you keep them dry, they'll keep your feet dry." This answer pleased Jimmy and he left a satisfied customer.

Doing The Donkey Walk

Joe Drum was infuriated. A malicious talebearer had told him that Tom McKay said that he walked like his donkey. This was fighting talk! Joe headed straight to McKay's house and found him working out in the back yard.

"Did you say that I walked like my donkey?"

"I said nothing of the kind."

"What did you say then?"

"All I said was that your donkey walked like you."

"Oh is that all? That's alright then!"

And with that he turned and went home.

The Convoy To Moville

Joe Drum was also famous for one of his great sayings.

Years ago the emigrants from Maghera district to America would walk, along with friends and family, to Moville in County Donegal to catch the trans-Atlantic boat. "The Convoy to Moville," as it became known, was a sad affair since those who were leaving would, in all likelihood, never see their native shores and loved ones again.

Joe Drum, ever eager to be helpful and wishing to ease the pain of the moment, pronounced a benediction as the emigrants were about to board the boat. He declared, "May God be with them that's going for I'll be with them that's staying."

Charlie the Mucker

Charlie the Mucker was very, very careful about his hair. He, however, came to a stage where he had only two hairs left on the top of his head, … and that was it. But he took care of them. Every morning he looked at them in the mirror with glowing admiration. But, one morning as he awakened, he looked down and saw the two hairs on top of the pillow and said, "My God! I'm bald!"

The Country Drive

Occasionally Willie and Bella were taken for a Sunday afternoon "spin" around the country in a friend's car. On one such drive they were passing by a large field when they noticed a curious donkey peering through the hedge.

" Look Willie," laughed Bella, "There's one of your relatives."

"It is indeed," agreed Willie, "but only by marriage."

The Other Side

A rather distraught looking man somewhat under the influence, approached Eoin Walsh and inquired as to where the other side of the street was located. "It's over there," said Eoin pointing across the road.

"My God," said the drunk, "that's very odd for Josie Martin told me it was over here."

The Wife's Doing a Line!

Willie Given was sitting one day in the hedge at Burns's Brae. In his hand he was holding two wee pebbles with which he kept gently tapping his head. Up comes Henry Hutchinson and says, "What are you doing there Willie Given?"

"I'm going to beat my brains in," says Willie in a low voice, "for the wife's doing a line with Johnny McKeown."

"And what," asks Henry, "are you going to use to beat your brains in with?"

"I'm going to do it way these," says Willie, showing Henry the pebbles.

"Ach those would be no good" says Hutchinson going over to the ditch and lifting out two big sharp stones.

"Here," he says, "try these."

Willie Given looked at the two big sharp stones and then looked at the two wee pebbles and said, "Ach, I don't think I'll bother the day."

The Government Post

Willie Murphy had been on the drink all day. It was now after 1 AM and the barman at O'Hara's had finally persuaded the patrons to leave. "Ach well" said Murphy "sure I might as well go home and warm my feet in front of a big roaring wife." So off he staggered down Main Street singing and shouting as he went. Just past Hall Street he felt he could go no farther without falling and as good fortune would have it there was a convenient lamppost around which he was able to wrap his arms.

Just then, his arch foe, Sergeant Murdoch, Maghera's Wyatt Earp, came round the corner and spied him gently swaying in the breeze supported only by the pole.

"Willie Murphy, what are you doing there?" roared Murdock

"Ach Sergeant" says Murphy, "much the same as yourself. I'm just trying to hold on to a government post."

The Temperance Lecture

Peacock O'Neil was a tall, very thin man with sharp features, a red face and a long nose…hence the nickname Peacock.

Peacock was stopped by Sergeant Murdoch around 2 AM and Murdoch asked him where he was going at that time of night. Peacock replied, "I am going to a lecture about alcohol abuse and the ill effects it has on the human body."

Murdoch then says, "Is that so? And who is giving that lecture at this time of night?"

Peacock replies, "That would be my wife."

For Better Or For Worse

Bella Murphy was having trouble with Willie. In her distress she went and asked Father Hegarty if he could give her any advice. "Well" says Father Hegarty, "You could, as Saint Paul taught, try kindness, thereby heaping coals of fire on his head."

"No Father that wouldn't do any good" says Bella, "for I tried scalding him once with water and that didn't work."

On another occasion Willie says to Bella, "I married you for life, but can I get time off for good behaviour?"

At one stage, Willie and Bella's marriage was, by all accounts, finished. Apparently there was no chance of reconciliation, at least that's what was being said. They had parted ways. Willie was sitting one day in his house when someone rapped the front door. On answering it, Willie was confronted by a concerned Father Duffy. Father Duffy began telling Willie how good a wife Bella had been. Accordingly, she had cooked, cleaned, and had kept the house very tidy. In short she was a lovely woman and he should take her back. "Well what do you think Willie?" asked Father Duffy. In typical Murphy style he replied, "Father if you think so much of her why don't you take her?"

Thanks to Pat Rafferty for the picture of Maghera

Rat's Birthday

Willie Murphy, when he had drink taken, became a great philosopher. He would often wax eloquent on current affairs, religion and local events. One night he was asked to propose a toast to Rat O'Neill on the occasion of Rat's birthday. Willie stood to his feet, raised his glass and said, "To what shall I compare our dear friend Rat? I can't compare him to the Sun for he's not that bright. I can't compare him to the Stars for they only come out at night and our friend Rat is on the go the whole time. And I can't compare him to the moon for the moon is full only part of the time while happily our friend Rat is full all of the time. To the incomparable Rat O'Neill, Happy Birthday!"

Gathering Spuds

 Willie Murphy was a hard worker when the notion came on him. He'd often do seasonal work for local farmers and one year he was hired by Old Man Marshall to help gather potatoes. However, this one particular day, old Marshall came along and sat down in the hedge. He just sat there for hours holding unto his walking stick staring at Willie and his co-worker. Willie didn't like this arrangement one little bit as it make him feel quite nervous and awkward. So eventually, Willie went over to him and asked, "Mr. Marshall, do you play draughts?" "Ach sure I do indeed," replied Old Man Marshall "why do you ask?

"Because," says Willie "if you don't soon make a move, you're about to lose two men."

The Puzzle Of The Travelling Bus

It was a wet kind of a day and a group of characters were gathered at Carson Caldwell's garage at the foot of the town. The craic was mighty when up speaks "Rambutt" Richardson and says, "Fellas, I've got a puzzle for you. There was this bus that left Maghera with thirty passengers on it and when it got to the Hill Head ten passengers got off and five got on. Are you following? Then it went on to Castledawson and six got off and nine got on. Are you following? When it came to Magherafelt nineteen passengers got off and fifteen got on. Are you with me?"

"Wait a minute wait a minute," says Charlie the Bare how many got off?"

"Nineteen got off."

"And how many got on?"

"Fifteen. Are you with me?"

Nods of approval.

"Then, the bus went on to Tobermore and seven got off and four got on.

Then it came back to Maghera and everybody got off."

"Now did you follow all that?" says Rambutt.

"We did," they all agreed.

"Good" say Rambutt "Now here's the question. Tell me, what was the name of the bus driver?"

Of course, no one knew the answer so Rambutt says, "His name was Brown."

"How do you get that?" says Dido McAtamney

"Because his Father's name was Brown."

Well they laughed and roared and lambasted 'Rambutt' for telling such a daft story. But they had to admit however that he'd 'got them.'

On into the afternoon they continued telling yarns and talking nonsense till a little later Willie Murphy joined their company. After a while, Jimmy the Spat says to Richardson, "Hi Rambutt, ask Willie to solve that puzzle you told earlier about the bus and see if Willie can work it out."

So Rambutt starts in, "There was this bus that left Maghera with thirty passengers." And so he began to spin his yarn taking the bus to the Hill Head on through Castledawson: With such and such a number getting off in Magherafelt and such and such a number in Tobermore and so on and so forth back to Maghera.

"Now Willie, Did you follow all that?" asks Rambutt when he had finished.

"I did indeed," says Murphy

" Now Willie here's the question. Tell me," and then he paused for effect, "what was the name of the driver?"

"I haven't got a clue."

"His name was Brown."

"How do you get that?"

"Because his Father's name was Brown"

Wait a minute, not so fast," says Murphy, "how could his name have possibly been Brown when according to your facts and figures there were only twenty-four people on the bus when it arrived in Tobermore?

A Pain In The?

Doctor Johnston had a patient who one-day complained about having a great pain in, 'his kidilies.'

"The word is kidneys, not kidilies," corrected Dr Johnston.

"Oh diddil I say kidilies?"

Collecting Bottles

When Willie Murphy was a wee lad, there was a common practice of charging a deposit for drinks that came in glass bottles. If you wanted a bottle of minerals (the forerunner of Coke, Pepsi and the like), you'd pay, not only for the mineral, but also pay for a small deposit on top of the purchase price. The deposit, of course, was given back when the bottle was returned. Young Willie, in his enterprising fits, would often make a few extra pennies by going about finding empty mineral bottles. He soon discovered likewise there was money to be made on empty whiskey bottles so he began knocking doors and asking people if they had any such bottles in their homes.

One day he knocked on the door of a well know religious lady. Says Willie to her, "Missus would you happen to have any auld whiskey bottles in there?" Well, she stood for a moment just glaring down at him with a face on her like a Sphinx. There she stood, arms folded, with her hair tied up in a bun with a great big pin sticking through it. Her long black dress smelt musty and old. Her eyes were cold and disapproving. Willie, for a moment, was quite unnerved.

"Do I look like a woman who drinks whiskey?" she sneered through her tight, thin lips.

Willie stood back, looked her up and down then says, "I suppose not. But tell me then, you wouldn't happen to have any empty vinegar bottles would you?"

The Medical Philosopher

A certain medical Doctor from Maghera, a gentleman from another generation who will remain nameless, was never known to refuse a drink. One night he was relaxing with a pint in Richardson's pub when someone said to him, "Have you no patients to see tonight Doctor."

A little the worse for wear, he replied, "Well Sammy it's like this, it doesn't matter whether I see them or not for I'll tell you the truth, half of them are so sick that all the Doctors in the world couldn't cure them and the other half are that strong that all the Doctors in the world couldn't kill them….so make mine a half one when you're ready."

The Solo

Socials were a great event in years gone by. A hall would be secured and an evening's entertainment would be arranged. Poems would be recited, songs sung and skits enacted and the whole district would converge for a night's craic.

At one such social in the Curragh Orange Hall, just outside Maghera, the evening was in full swing when the Master of Ceremonies announced, "And now Ladies and Gentlemen, Miss Maisy McFarland will sing us a solo."

Suddenly, a loud voice from the back of the hall hurled the startling words, "Maisy McFarland's nothing but an auld bitch."

Instantly the M.C. responded, "Nevertheless, Miss Maisy McFarland will now sing us a solo."

Run, Run Quick, Quick Run!

At Roger's Barber Shop, in Hall Street, a man was sitting in the chair having his hair cut when suddenly the door bursts open and a man runs in shouting, "Run, quick Mr. Smith, run quick, your house is on fire."

The man jumps off the chair, runs out the door, towels and all, and flies like the hammers away down Hall Street and then suddenly stops and says, "What am I running for, sure my name's not Smith."

Politicians

"What do you think of our politicians?" asked Stick Leg. "Well," says Willie, "when it comes to politicians, one man is as good as another and, for that matter, very often a great deal better."

The Illicit Liquor by William Burns

Some men we knew made mountain dew,

(Poteen's its other name)

Although it was against the law,

They made both wealth and fame.

The word was passed by nod of head,

Or even a wink would do,

For those who wished to get a taste

Of this most potent brew.

The place to find a private still,

Was moor or mountainside,

For if the police should make a raid,

It gave some time to hide.

One day when Pat was in the fair -

He came from the mountain top.

He had just started off for home,

When the sergeant made him stop.

'Now Pat you know the mountain well,

Just tell me if you will,

Are you aware of any place

Where there is a private still?'

'Oh yes indeed I do know one,

I'll take you to the place,

But as the distance is quite long,

We will keep a steady pace.'

The sergeant found the mountain climb

Both long and very hard

But was prepared to stick it out

To get his just reward

At last just further up the hill

They saw a cottage light,

And to the tired sergeant now

It was a pleasant sight.

As they approached the cottage gate

Said Pat 'Make little noise!

The last thing that we want to do

Is to disturb the boys.

If you come to this window here,

You'll get a better view.

Now everything I've told you

I'll promise will be true.

You see that man beside the fire,

To work he has got no will.

He is in the army twenty years,

And is a private still.'

The Small Religious

Object

Eoin Walsh, author of the marvellous little book, 'Famous Men of Maghera', was not very tall. In these days of political correctness we would probably say he was 'vertically challenged.' However, never having heard of 'political correctness', there were those in Maghera who said that he was 'that small he could do a handstand under the kitchen sink.' Still others said 'he wouldn't be eleven feet tall, even if he stood on top of a six-foot ladder.'

However, what he lacked in stature he made up for in wit, charm and religious zeal. A devout Roman Catholic, he often attended Mass every day and rarely missed any event in the Chapel. The following yarn was told by Eoin to one of his Protestant friends.

"Last night we had a mission at the Chapel," he said, "and the visiting priest was stirring us up to fever pitch when he said, 'now everybody hold up a small religious object'; and the man to my right just turned around and held me up above his shoulders."

Wild West Willie

When Willie Murphy was getting on in years the young lads used to talk to him to see if they could get any stories and auld yarns.

One day he told a group of them, "You probably don't know this lads, but when I was a very young man I emigrated to the States and went out West. One day, when minding my own business, Apaches attacked me. But I didn't worry too much because I had a fine horse and I thought I could probably out run them. However they kept gaining on me so I headed up a canyon and took cover behind some rocks. I wasn't too worried because I had a repeating rifle and plenty of shells so I kept emptying my bullets into them. I eventually ran out of bullets, but I wasn't too worried because I had a pair of six guns and plenty of ammo, but to my horror I eventually discovered that my bullets had run out and they were still coming at me. Twenty Apaches rushed me and I didn't have so much as a pen knife to defend myself."

Then Willie stopped talking and sat there in silence speaking nary a word. Eventually one of the lads spoke up and said, "Well what happened next Willie?"

"Why they killed me, of course. Curse them for a pack of savages, they killed me."

The Business Rivals

There was always a great rivalry between Jack Scott and Tom McKinney each of whom owned large businesses in Maghera. They vied with each other in many ways. Before the days of motorways or enforced speed limits, Jack and Tom used to race each other to Belfast on Thursdays. One day they met each other at Nuts Corner Airport (the forerunner of Aldergrove).

"Where are you going to today?" asks McKinney. Jack Scott hesitated then said, "I'm going to Manchester."

"You're such a liar Scott," McKinney said as he got all flustered. "You're telling me you are going to Manchester to make me think that you're going to Glasgow, but I've made inquiries and I know you really are going to Manchester."

The Auctioneer

Bull Bradley was a publican and auctioneer many years ago in Maghera. His main rival in the auctioneering trade was Bob Crawford and one day they happened to meet at the Bank Square.

"Bull," says Bob, "I had a dream last night and you were in it"

"I was?"

"Yes indeed. I dreamed I died and was waiting in line to get into Heaven.

"Boys a dear is that a fact?" says Bull.

"Indeed it is," says Bob. "There was Saint Peter standing with his long white beard interviewing everyone who was trying to get in, and to my shock I saw you standing up ahead of me in the line. When you got up to Saint Peter, he says to you, "What's your name?" and you replied, bold as you like, "Bull Bradley."

Then St Peter says, "Where are you from?"

"I'm from Maghera," you replied with a swell in your chest.

"Occupation?"

"I'm an auctioneer," you said proudly.

"Welcome to Heaven," says St Peter, "go on, on in."

"Well this gave me some hope when I saw how easy it was for you," says Bob, "so when my turn came, St. Peter looks at me and says,

"Name?"

"Bob Crawford."

"Where from?"

"Maghera."

'Occupation?"

"Auctioneer."

"I'm sorry Mr. Crawford," says St. Peter but we don't allow auctioneers in here."

"Wait a minute," says I, "I saw you letting Bull Bradley in just a moment ago."

"Ach, now, now Mr. Crawford," says St Peter "Sure everybody knows Bull Bradley's no auctioneer."

Bob Crawford and Bull Bradley bumped into each other one day in Magherafelt and Bob, trying to be smart, said, " Now where in hell have I seen you before?"

"That all depends," said Bull. "Whereabouts in Hell do you come from?"

The Only way To Travel

Rat O'Neill a small, thin man always claimed to be descended from the Royal O'Neills and although he was from the Market Yard, he always spoke with a posh accent. On account of this, he was often referred to as Lord O'Neill. One day, in Belfast, he was going into York Street Station to catch the train back to Maghera.

He had expected his brothers Roper and Tossley to make the journey to Belfast with him, but at the last minute they had had a change of plans. Rat was feeling quite melancholy and lonely when up comes Charlie the Bare and says, "Rat can you help me? I'm flat broke and I need the price of a ticket to get home." "Well," says Rat, "I'm pretty broke myself, but I'll tell you what I'll do. You get into the same carriage as me and hide under the seat and I'll cover you with my legs."

This then was agreed and Rat, unknown to Charlie, went off and bought two tickets to Maghera. The train pulled out of the station and Charlie, as agreed, hid under the seat making himself as comfortable as possible. Eventually the conductor came around and Rat gave him the two tickets.

"And where's the other passenger?" asked the conductor.

Rat tapped his forehead, gave the conductor a knowing look, and said with his polished accent, "That's my friend's ticket. You see he's somewhat eccentric and prefers to travel on the floor."

The Price Of A Pint

Old Archie Mac was a harmless soul, but very fond of the drink. Always thirsty, he had the reputation of often being "on the tap." In other words he didn't mind asking people for a few bob to help quench his thirst. One day he met Mickey Bryson, who had a reputation of being a man exceedingly difficult to separate from his money.

"I saw your photo in the paper the other day," says Archie

"You did, did you?" says Bryson "and I suppose you asked the photo for the price of a drink?"

"Ach not at all" said Archie "The picture was such a perfect likeness of yourself that I knew there'd be no point."

The Night Of The Long Knives

Murphy and the boys had been getting fed up with Mickey Bryson. His meanness, when it came to money, knew no bounds. Mickey was the kind of man who when it came to giving, stopped at nothing. They used to joke about him saying that he went to Belfast one day and a robber stuck a gun to his face saying, "your money or your life." There was a long pause. The gunman snarled, "Well?"

Mickey said, "Don't rush me! I'm thinking about it."

In the pub, Mickey was the sort who was always available if you wanted to stand a round, but when his round came he'd mysteriously disappear. He was, as Niall Toibin said of an acquaintance, "A secular version of the immaculate conception for he became an alcoholic without ever buying a drink."

So a plan was hatched to give him a right 'sickener'. Mickey was cordially invited to a night of drinking at Sam Stockman's entry, (then located at the bottom of Hall Street). The bottles were passed and the craic began. Mickey, however, didn't notice that every time the bottle was passed to him the lads were letting him drink out of a specially concocted bottle of mixed cheap wine and rot-gut spirits. Eventually the concoction began to produce the desired effect and Mickey began to feel ill. But since the drink was free, Bryson, on a point of principle, kept on guzzling. Eventually he could take no more and went over to the corner and began to 'heave up.' "Oh Lord," he cried as he wretched, "I offer this up for the sins of the world." He vomited a second time and again petitioned, "Oh Lord I offer this up for the suffering in the world." Stick Leg turned in disgust to Murphy and the rest of the lads and quipped, "My God boys, look at that, he's that mean he'd let nothing go to waste."

The Builders

Two men we had when I was young,

To do a house repair:

Willie John the builder's mate,

And Matt beyond compare.

As a builder of both stone and brick,

He had won a great renown,

And what he built is still admired,

In many a country town.

Now Willie John was very glad,

To help his building skill,

And had a very great desire,

An ambition to fulfill

To build some dwelling on his own,

That people could admire.

He even spoke to Matt himself,

About his great desire.

Said Matt 'The pig house must be built,

You cannot do much wrong,

I'll let you build the house yourself,

If you don't take too long.'

It wasn't long til Willie John,

Had the foundation made,

For he was good at manual work,

And digging with the spade.

The day was hot and Matthew took

The straw hat from his head

And as he still was very warm

His coat he also shed.

When everybody's back was turned

A sow was passing by

Who up to then, It was assumed,

Was closed inside the sty.

Although she had other things to eat

She went for Matt's straw hat

And when the last straw was devoured

Was not content with that,

But started chewing at the coat

She saw upon the ground

And half a sleeve had disappeared

When Matthew turned around.

Matt chased the pig and got his coat

But when he put it on

You could have heard a mile away

The laughs of Willie John.

Matthew was raging with the sow

As well as Willie John

And didn't know on which to rack

His greater vengeance on.

Whilst Willie John was wondering

What style his house would be

Whether it would be Georgian

Or just plain ordinary

And then the great day had arrived -

The pig house was complete

And Willie John brought Matthew

For his verdict on his feat.

Matthew stared and then he spoke

With a voice both loud and slow

'you've put the window upside down

But the pigs will never know'.

By **William Burns**

Making Her Mark

Clara Stewart, a big barrel of a woman, never learned to read or write properly so when she had to sign anything, to save embarrassment, she simply made an X. One time a parcel arrived for her and instead of the customary X she made an O. The postman was a wee bit confused and said "Clara what happened to your normal signature? Why did you put an O instead of an X? "Ach Jimmy, I thought you knew," says Clara "I got married last Saturday and I had to change my name."

An interesting fact about Clara is that when she did get married to Willie Stewart she didn't know that he was bald until the day of the wedding and that's only because he had to take his cap off in the church.

Clara had almost married someone called Willie Crossett and when she and her husband were not getting on, she would throw up this fact to her long suffering spouse. You see, she and Willie Stewart had only one daughter, Tilly, and she would jibe that if she had married Willie Crossett she would be now lifting over 25 shillings in children's allowance.

Clara saw everything that was going on around her and more besides. She and Willie lived in what was known as the 'Front

Street' and Clara used to hang over the half door and call out her diagnosis of everyone who was en route to Dr. Johnston's surgery.

One day, from her vantage point she looked over to the Church School during lunch break and noticed a wee boy crying because he had left his lunch inside the school. The poor wee lad couldn't get back into the school because the school Principal, Mr. McGarvey, a man much given to amorous dalliances had, allegedly, locked the door. So Clara went to investigate and realised what was going on. As bold as brass, she knocked on the school door and said........listen here McGarvey....I have not come here to know what you and that woman are up to, I am just here to get the hungry wane its piece (sandwich).

One day Clara went to see Dr. Johnston. Says the good Doctor, "Clara we haven't seen you in here for a while"

"Ach, I know," says Clara, "Sure I haven't been very well lately."

Confusion Twice Confounded

(Tirnoney Dolmen, Maghera)

A very well meaning gentleman was trying to get Willie Murphy to amend his ways. He reasoned with him about temperance and the evils of drink. "Deed aye, you're right, I agree with you entirely," says Murphy, "but perhaps you don't know that the only reason I drink is to forget my childhood"

"Your childhood?"

"Yes, my childhood. You see very few people know that, when I was young, we lived up at Tirnoney near the dolmen. I was a twin and no one, not even my dear old mother, God rest her, could tell us apart. Well, me brother and I were playing outside one evening and my Da was coming into the yard with the horse and cart. Suddenly the horse bolted and ran over one of us. Now this is where my difficulties started. Everybody thought it was my brother who was killed and I was the one who lived. But I was the one that was killed and my brother the one who lived and ever since then, the only thing that gives me any comfort is the drink.

The Airplane

Back in the 1950s, it was a rare thing to see an airplane high up in the skies above Maghera. There just was not the same amount of air travel back then. One day, Willie was walking down the street when he espies Father Hegarty standing at the top of Hall Street looking up in the air. Murphy stopped beside him and gazed heavenward just in time to see a distant airplane. Father Hegarty says, "Willie, I'm glad I'm not up there in one of those."

Murphy replies, "Well Father, I'm glad I'm not up there and not in one of those."

'Stick Leg' McMurray on the left (with thanks to William Cunningham)

Modern Art

Stick Leg Mc Murray and Willie Murphy were talking one night and the subject turned to modern art.

"What do you think of this boyo Picasso?" asks Stick Leg.

"Ach I don't know a lot about him" says Willie "but he's obviously a deeply spiritual man."

"What makes you think that?

"Well the Bible says we are not to make unto ourselves the likeness of any living thing that is in Heaven or on earth or in the waters under the earth; and your man Picasso has obeyed that to a tee."

Passing Wind

Willie Murphy, in his boyhood schooldays, was sitting in class when the teacher, Miss Bradley, accidentally farted. Willie began to laugh and the embarrassed teacher threatened, "You stop that at once Willie Murphy."

"Ach Mamm I can't," says Willie "sure it's half way down the road by now."

Now That's Cold!

Willie Murphy, Stick Leg McMurray and Charlie the Bare were talking about how cold the day was. In fact, they agreed that it was one of the coldest days they had ever experienced.

Stick Leg then said, "Mind you boys, it's not near as cold as it was one winter in the trenches in France for it was that cold wan day with the wind blowing up me arse that I was farting snowflakes till June."

"Ach," says Charlie the Bare, "That's nothing! I remember one winter I was working up in a field beyond Dungiven and it was that cold that when I went to have a pee, me pee froze solid in mid air, and when I was finished, I had to break it off just to get me trousers buttoned."

"Sure that's nothing," says Murphy, "I remember one winter morning when Bella and I woke up, it was so cold that as we spoke, the words came out of our mouths frozen solid. Well, we hadn't got a clue what we were saying to each other, so we had to boil up a pot of water and put the words in to thaw them out so that we could understand what we were on about.

A Bad Case Of Ulsters

Carson Caldwell shuffled in to see Joe Burns one day. Up the long stairs he went to the office and was almost out of breath by the time he reached the top. How are you Carson? asked Mr. Burns. Unfortunately, Carson never having heard the age old truth, "Tell not your friends of your indigestion; 'how are you doing?' is a greeting, not a question," launched into a monologue about his ailing health. Here's how it ended;

" Aye and you know Joe, I'm far from well. I'm very bad way the auld stomach as well. I was away at the Doctors and he says I'm very bad. He says I've got Ulsters in me stomach. Aye, that's what he said, I'm bad way the Ulsters."

Your Brave Warm Work

It was a cold dark winter's morning in Upperlands and the rain was spitting against the windows of Tommy's house. The alarm clock had gone off for the second time. Outside the wind was howling with threatening menace. Tommy turned over on his side and said to the wife, "You go on to your brave warm work and I'll try and stick it out here 'til lunch time."

A Man With A Mission

'Wully' S was a harmless decent man, but a character in some ways. Take for example the night his wife, Mrs. S, was giving birth to her sixth child. The midwife had come to render assistance and Mrs. S was now having ever closer contractions. It was just past eleven at night so Wully climbs into the bed and gets under the covers.

"Mr. S," protests the midwife "you need to get up out of that for your wife's about to give birth."

"Deed not," says Wully "I need my sleep. I've got to get up the morra to gather spuds." And with that, he turned over, and calmly nodded off. Mr. S remained in bed for the rest of the night while, lying beside him, Mrs S added a bouncing baby boy to their already substantial brood.

The Plural Of Last?

Alfie Kilpatrick was a Saddler by trade but he thought he might diversify into cobbling shoes. So he decided to send off for two cobblers lasts and composed a note to the manufacturer. "Dear Sirs" it read, "Please send me two lasts." Reading what he had written he thought perhaps something was wrong. What would the plural of last be? Was lasts really the correct word? Just then the John Joe, the Fairy Campbell came in and Alfie says to him "John Joe, what's the plural of last, as in cobblers last? Would it be cobbler's lasts?"

"Muum humm" says Fairy Campbell. (No one knew why he did it, but the Fairy always started his sentences by saying Muum humm)

"Muum humm" says Fairy and then with his pronounced lisp said, "I sthink thatss it'ss lastae or lastee or ssome kind of Latin construction."

Alfie was still unconvinced so he wrote, "Dear sirs, Please send me a cobblers last and while you're at it, please send me another one."

Out Of The Will

Archie Mac, unhappy at his son's behaviour, threatened to not even leave him so much as a shilling in his will. His son immediately replied, "But Da, where would you borrow the shilling?"

Murphy and the Train

"Did you miss the train Willie?"

"No, not a bit of me. I didn't like the look of it, so I chased it out of the station."

The Solution

Willie Murphy met Dr. Love on the Main Street one afternoon and said, "Doctor, something is badly wrong. When I get up in the morning I have dizziness for half an hour and then I feel great." What should I do?"

"Get up later!," replied Dr. Love.

The Magical Mystery Tour

A.E. and N, both now deceased, spent their entire lives in Maghera. In their retirement days they loved to get out and about and "see round them" as they visited various places. One day, while at 'The Port', they saw an advertisement for, 'The Magical Mystery Tour.' Accordingly, there was a bus that would take its passengers to mysterious and exotic destinations within driving range of Portrush. So, being assured by the driver that they would be back in good time, they paid their tickets and got on-board.

The bus was well filled and our two friends engaged in light hearted conversation with each other thus ensuring that their journey would feel much shortened. Eventually the destination was reached and, as the excited passengers disembarked, the two friends looked out of the window only to discover that the Magical Mystery Tour had taken them to, well you've guessed it, Maghera. They were mortified, and sat hiding in the bus in case anyone from Maghera would see them.

The Wee Folk of Belfast

My Granny Burns didn't often get out and about to places other than Maghera. But one day, my Uncle Evan took her to Belfast, 'to the pictures'. The next evening she was telling the story of her big day out in Belfast. James Haire, the Presbyterian minister was one of their guests this particular evening. Granny was in full articulate flow, describing the length of the cinema queue and the people standing in it when she said, "As I looked around, I noticed that Belfast is just full of wee men. As I looked at that queue I never saw so many wee men in all my life." Suddenly, the scales dropped from her eyes. She was describing the Revd Dr James Haire, a man famed for his pocket size stature. On top of that, he was from Belfast. Well, having never heard the ancient maxim that 'when you're in a hole stop digging' she hurriedly said, "Just children you know, just children, it's a wonder their mothers let them out so late."

Tom O'Halloran

Tom O'Halloran was a well know vagrant beggar in the 1940s. When in the district, he often called with my Grandparents at the Mullagh, just outside of Maghera. They always gave him a good meal and a bed for the night.

Tom claimed descent from the "Auld Kings" and he could have been right for the O'Hallorans ruled a Kingdom in the Galway area before the Norman invasion of Ireland. They had been aristocrats who, in the course of many upheavals, had ended up as landless peasantry. This may have been what happened to Tom's branch of the family.

The story of Noah and his ark is in Genesis 5:29 - 10:32

One evening Tom was present at Family Worship at the Mullagh. It so happened that the passage of Scripture my Grandfather was reading was about Noah and the Flood. Tom suddenly pipes up and asks, "Is there no mention of the O'Hallorans there."

"I'm afraid not," said Granny Burns.

Then says Tom, "I should have known that, for the O'Hallorans were always a very proud lot and would have had their own boat."

Willie Groggan

Great Uncle Robert had a man, Willie Groggan, who worked for him on the farm. Willie was know as one of the strongest men in the district and a tremendously hard worker. One day, Great Uncle Robert had to go into Maghera on some errand or other so he said to Willie, "When I'm gone I want you to go in and clean out the barn and then clean out the byre. Then I want you to snedd the turnips and weed the vegetables and paint the front door of the house and clean all the gutters at the back of the house and fix those lose slates on the roof. Willie took off his cap and rubbed his forehead and asked, "And tell me Mr. Burns, what do you want me to do with the snow?"

"Snow? Sure there's no snow at this time of year Willie."

"Aye, but there will be by the time I get through with all that!"

Don't Be Nebulous!

Many years ago, when I was a drinking lad, I was sitting in McMasters pub along with my good friend William "Billy" Graham. The door swung open and in walked Roy Shiels, playwright and raconteur par excellence. Says Roy, "Hello young McKee. Hello young Graham how are you two tonight?

"Great ," we replied. Then says Billy, "What are you having Roy?"

"Well I'm feeling nebulous."

"Yes but what are you having?"

"I'm feeling nebulous" repeated Roy

"Yes but what do you want to drink?"

"Do you not know what nebulous means?" says Roy

We hadn't a clue!

"Boys a dear," says Roy, and the two of you educated young pups. Get yourself a good dictionary and look up 'Nebulous' and you'll see that it means 'Vague.' So don't be vague, ask for Haig.

Guttyass McKenna

George Barnett was walking out of Draperstown one day when he encountered the infamous Mr. Guttyass McKenna. Just so that you'll understand the name 'Guttyass', it seems that the McKennas in those days were so numerous that most of them had nicknames to distinguish them one from the other. Guttyass had not always been so named. Apparently, when he was a wee lad, he had come in from school one day with the backside torn out of his trousers. His mother, being the thrifty sort, took an old gutty (an ancient version of the training shoe or runner), melted down the sole and patched his trousers. From that day on till the day he died Patrick Joseph McKenna was simply known as Guttyass.

Now back to the story. George Barnett meets Guttyass and after exchanging the usual civilities said,

"Guttyass, you come from a remarkable family."

"Do you think so?"

"Aye, I do indeed!"

"And why's would that be?"

"Well first of all, your Mother saw the Ghost of the Carn."

"Aye, deed she did."

And your wife, sure she saw the fairies dancing at Lough Fea."

"Aye deed so."

"And your daughter, she saw the Virgin Mary at Ardboe."

"Aye, boys that's right indeed."

" How come it is then," says George "that not one of you have seen your cows in my corn for this last two weeks?"

Pin McDonald And The Flying Missile

When Pin McDonald, the tailor, was a young lad a few of his friends had gathered at the Bank Square. They began to tell yarns and stories and the craic was mighty. But, by now, it was getting late and Pin had to go home as his mother was unwell. So he says, "Come on lads we'll call it a night."

But no one stirred. The craic was too good. And Pin, well he didn't want to go home and miss out on anything so he stayed a while longer. Then he being, once more, urged by the silent call of filial duties said, "Ah fellas, it's getting late, sure we'll call it a day."

Again no one stirred.

Just then Pin lifted a big stone and hurled it through a window smashing it to pieces. Then Pin looked around at them and said, "I howl yees boys, yees 'ill go home now."

Willie And The Raging Bull

One day Bella sent Willie over to Marshall's farm to buy some eggs. It was a nice sort of a day, so on the way home Willie thought he would take a short cut across the fields. Little did he know, however, that he was now in the domain of Marshall's prize bull; and Marshall's bull, not being endowed with many social graces, took a rather dim view of trespassers.

All was going well till the bull spied Murphy and charged. Willie hadn't realized he still could run so swiftly, but when the bull ran at him, he took to his feet like ten men and a wee fella and just managed to get over the gate thus avoiding the full force of bovine wrath.

Alas, however, the eggs did not enjoy the same measure of success and survival.

They didn't even made it to the gate as they were thrown heavenward by Willie, as he sought to find some extra speed: And Willie thus had to return empty handed to a domestic scene dominated by a somewhat less than tranquil bliss.

"Where's the eggs?" demanded Bella.

"Marshall's bull got them."

"What would an auld bull want way a dozen eggs?

"Well I don't mean he got them to eat for his lunch, but he'd have eaten me if he'd caught up with me."

"So he chased you out of the field."

"Aye."

"You let him chase you out of the field and him just a slip of an auld bull! A poor dumb beast that wouldn't hurt a fly frightened you…. You eegit you! What are you made of at all William Murphy? Are you a man or a mouse?"

Well she lambasted him and called him for all the auld turf men in the country, till he finally ' got all riz' and off he went armed with a big stick to take revenge on Marshall's bull. Climbing into the field and retracing his footsteps, however, he found no sign of his foe, but instead spied a few young calves in the corner down of the field down by the hedge. So Willie charged like a warrior of old into the midst of the fray striking the calves with a few stout blows. Of course they scattered so Willie called after them, "Go home now, go home and tell that father of yours what kind of a man Willie Murphy is."

The Times Of London

Years ago Hurley Curley had a wee shop on the Main Street of Maghera Now they say that God loves a trier and if that is so, He must have held a special place for Hurley Curley for she would have tried selling just about anything in that wee shop of hers. She tried selling it all, sweeties, toilet paper, soap, coal and turf …. You name it, she had it or would try to get it.

  Eventually she decided to expand into National Newspapers. One day Major Clark came in and said in his pronounced upper crust accent,

"Can I obtain a copy of the Times of London here?"

"Of course you can, we stock everything. Now tell me, would that be today's Times or yesterday's you'd be after?"

"Today's or yesterday's?" he said with a raised and surprised voice. "What use would I have for yesterday's paper? It's today's paper I want of course."

"Well then, if it's today's paper you want, come back tomorrow."

The Source

On another occasion Mickey Shoddy went in to Hurley Curley's and asked for a newspaper to which Mrs. Hurley Curley replied, "Why, what is it you want to know?"

Barney Devlin

Barney Devlin had a wee shop in the town. He sold all manner of things and was, "All things to all men." One popular item he carried was a picture of a 17th century soldier crossing a river on a white horse. When a unionist customer inquired about it, he would persuade them that it was a picture of King Billy at the Boyne. When a Nationalist customer inquired about the same picture, he would persuade them it was Sarsfield at Limerick.

Jassy Brown and Mrs. Noone

Mrs Noone and her husband Willie ran a prosperous grocery shop in Maghera. Mrs. Noone, a decent woman, was one of the thinnest women in the country. In fact, some Maghera folk used to say that she'd gone into hospital to have her varicose veins removed, but the hospital made a mistake and removed her legs, but left the veins.

One day, Jassy Brown went into her shop. Now Jassy had a wee dog that followed him everywhere and true to form, the wee dog was right there with him.

"Jassy Brown," calls out Mrs. Noone, can't you read the sign. It says 'No Dogs Allowed'.

"Oh I can read well enough Mrs. Noone," says Jassy, "but the poor wee dog can't read a word.

The Tullyheron Ghost

McFalone was his name and I used to see him around the town often enough. He lived up in Tullyheron and was known as 'The Ghost' for no more sinister a reason than his skin could have been the inspiration for Procol Harum's, "A Whiter Sade of Pale." 'The Ghost' had grown up on a wee farm and was the youngest of a large family. He had been, by all accounts, a sickly child. By the time he grew up, most, if not all, of his siblings had joined the emigrant trail and had arrived and settled in America. As a result, "The Ghost" was, apart from his ageing widowed mother, the only one left at home. It seems 'The Ghost' never worked nor could work because of poor health. In her wisdom, therefore, before his mother died, Mrs McFalone arranged with the sisters in America that money would be sent home each month to ensure 'The Ghost' would be able to keep both body and soul together.

Several years had elapsed since his mother's passing and things had slowly become worse for McFalone. His days were spent walking into town and going to the Library where he would sit quietly and read. But his health kept quietly ebbing away. His acquaintances began to notice his decline and it was decided that part of the problem was that 'The Ghost' was suffering from malnutrition as a result of doing his own cooking. And when it was further discovered that each month there was money from

America, his friends urged him to go to Walsh's Hotel where he could enjoy at least one substantial meal per day. After all, he could well afford it and why wouldn't he since it would be a big improvement on his staple diet of tea and toast?

Walsh's hotel in bygone days

So off to Walsh's he went for his lunch. It was a big event. It was his first time in a restaurant. There he sat reading the menu with great relish and anticipation. Then the waitress came to take his order and the poor Ghost froze.

"What can I get you?" inquired the waitress.

The Ghost just sat there saying nothing.

"What do you want to order?" came the polite inquiry.

Again the Ghost sat in a state of apparent paralysis, but now his normally pale cheeks were turning bright red with embarrassment.

"Can I take your order?" she inquired a third time.

By this time, the Ghost didn't know which way to look. You see, he hadn't expected a female to take his order. He was mortified and sat there wondering what to do. He thought the whole matter somewhat indelicate so finally with a feeble, nervous and embarrassed voice he said,

"Could I have a chest of chicken and chips please?"

Herbie Cunningham

Herbie Cunningham was a great fiddler and singer. He knew all the 'auld' songs and would sing them when doing his work. One day at The Mullagh, my grandparents farm just outside Maghera, my Uncle Bill, then a young lad, was designated as Herbie's helper. As the day progressed Uncle Bill listened, with great amusement and merriment, to Herbie's singing. Cunningham broke into one old song declaring something like,

"The Orange men did climb the glen,

One morning in July;

When all at once they were ascunced,

When Fenians they did spy!"

Uncle Bill burst out laughing and Herbie, quick as a flash, ceasing his chanting, gave Uncle Bill a hard stare. Then with all seriousness, he looked Uncle Bill straight in the eye and said, "You shouldn't laugh at that, that's an Orange Song. That's near the same as a hymn."

The Need of The Hour

Stick Leg McMurray, Willie Murphy and Bill Kearney were walking down the main Street in Maghera when Stick Leg slipped and fell with the result that his wooden leg came off.

"Are you hurt? Are you hurt?" says Kearney.

Do you need a doctor?" says Murphy.

"Ach" says Stick Leg, "It's not a Doctor I need, it's a bloody carpenter."

The Blind Pension

Charlie the Mucker was a man who felt that his call in life was to consume copious amounts of alcohol. The only trouble was that he rarely had enough money to pursue his vocation with the due diligence and dedication that such a high calling demanded. He thought, therefore, he should apply for the 'Blind Pension.' The trouble was, however, that he wasn't blind. But not to be deterred he took the application form to Freddy Tohill and asked him to complete it for him. Freddy obliged and when it came to the section asking for details on the blindness, Freddy wrote, "Blind for three days each week."

The Diagnosis

Archie Mac was a well meaning, uncomplicated man. One day he was in Tohill's, the Butchers, and complained to Freddy Tohill about not feeling well.

"Tell me exactly how you feel," says Freddie "What are your symptoms?"

"Ach," says Archie "my tummy is kind of queasy and sore all at the same time."

"Ach," says Freddie, "Sure I know what's the matter with you."

"You do?"

"Yes indeed I do. I'd know those symptoms anywhere."

"Well what's wrong with me?"

"You're pregnant," says Freddy.

"Pregnant! ….My God what does that mean?"

"Well you'd best go next door to Johnny Walsh the Chemist and ask him has he anything for it."

So off Archie Mac trots next door to speak to Mr. Walsh.

"Excuse me Mr. Walsh," says Archie, "but do you have a bottle you could give me, for you see I'm pregnant."

"You're pregnant?"

"Aye indeed Mr. Walsh."

"And who told you that you were pregnant?"

"Freddie Tohill."

"Well if Freddie Tohill diagnosed it you'd better go back to him and let him cure you."

Note from a Customer

'Dear Mr. Tohill, please send down a bone for soup for I am not well. I am in bed under the doctor and two sausages.'

The Front Garden

Willie Murphy and Bella moved from Church Street to a new bungalow. It was a cozy wee place, but it had a front garden that needed to be maintained. This did not suit Willie, as such maintenance would impose upon his busy drinking and social schedule. After a year the place looked like a small jungle was growing up to the front door and Father Duffy complained to Willie one day,

"Willie, this is ridiculous, you ought to take care of the things God gives you."

"True Father," says Willie, "It's like this, God gave me the garden, but I in turn gave it to the Devil and between the two of us we have let it go to Hell."

The 12th of July

It was the 12th of July in the evening and the Orangemen were returning from the field. Willie Murphy, a Roman Catholic, was standing by his front door when one of his Protestant neighbours, bedecked in Orange regalia, came staggering home.

"How did you get on today Sammy," asks Willie.

"We'd a great day, aye we did indeed, we kicked the Pope up and down the field."

"Serves him right," say Willie, "for he'd no business being

there in the first place."

The 12th in Tobermore

Richardson's pub was packed. It was the time when the faithful Orange men and loyal Christian brethren were in "The Field" listening to the speeches and sermon. However, the clientele in Richardson's that day were not known for being gospel greedy, … a 'lock of pints and half wans' being more to their taste. Suddenly, the door burst open and an irate man rushes in and shouts at the top of his angry voice, "Who hit the Fifer from the Culnady Lodge?"

Silence,

Maghera Orangemen and Band 1955. With thanks to Stephen Richardson.

Fists clenched and face turning ever redder he demanded again, "Who hit the Fifer from the Culnady Lodge?"

Silence

Just then, a big brute of a man who had been sitting quietly in the corner stood up and said, "I did."

The indignant man sized the brute up and down, unclenched his fists and said, "Well, I just thought I'd tell ye that ye hit him a quare good blow."

The Travelling Drapery Boy

My Great Uncle Joseph had a drapery shop on the main street of Maghera. For a time, a young chap named Hughie Leacock worked for him. One day, however, young Hughie handed in his notice saying that he wanted to see a bit of the world. The day came and he said his goodbyes and went on his way. Not long afterwards, a telegram arrived with the following words ."Have arrived safely at Knockloughrim." Man had he travelled!

A Longer Day

Charlie the Bare, when he was younger, met the commercial travellers getting off the train and carried their luggage to Walsh's Hotel. He got the nickname "Bare" because he mostly walked around in his bare feet. In later life, Charlie and hard work became perfect strangers. That's not to say that Charlie would lie in bed all day. In fact it was quite the opposite for he was a man much given to, 'rising with the lark.' And unlike Mark Twain, who boasted that he 'rose with the lark every morning, but fortunately owned an old lark that he had taught to sleep in', Charlie preferred to rise a long time before the dawn. Murphy questioned 'The Bare' about this habit seeing that he didn't go to work and got Charlie's excellent explanation that he liked to rise early for it gave him a longer day in which to do nothing.

McIntyre's Horse

Tommy McIntyre had three fields to plough with an old tired horse. Just as he finished ploughing the last field the old horse fell over and died. Tommy was, with sadness, relating the days events to a neighbour, Hughie Paul, and Hughie philosophically said, "Boys a dear, It's a good thing thon auld horse did what he done before he done what he did!"

Lazy to the Bone

The McConaghy family were known to be bone idle and lazy. They would have been morning people, if morning had happened around noon or one o'clock. Their wee cottage had a thatched roof which leaked and rather than repair it they slept in barrels at night to stop them getting soaked by the rain. When asked if they had any trouble with the Mayfly affecting their turnips, they said no, because they sowed the seed in June.

One of them once wanted to join the B Specials and was asked to bring a picture of himself. He didn't bother getting his picture taken, but cut out a picture of some random person in the Christian Herald and took it along. "That's not your picture," says the recruitment officer. "I know," said young McConakey, "but don't you think it's a brave wee likeness."

APPELLANTS AND PEELERS

The Light In The Window

During World War II, in Belfast, wee Billy Nelson, cap in hands, stood in the dock accused of violating the blackout by having a light shining in his window. His accuser, a big Peeler, said to the judge,

" And also your Honour, he gave me back cheek."

"Back cheek! Back cheek!" said the Judge as his face took on a look of doom. Sternly he asked wee Billy what he had to say for himself.

Your Honour" said wee Billy, "I never gave him any back cheek. He come to my door and said that I'd got a light in my window, and I said I hadn't. And then he said till step out here and see. So

I stepped out and looked and all I said to him was that if the German man landed his plane on the street and came over here to this window and struck a match he still couldn't have seen thon wee light. That's all I said, but I never gave him any back cheek."

How Davy Magee Took Stalingrad

In Belfast, during the Second World War, just off the Albert Bridge Road, in an area known as the Klondike, stood a pub nicknamed by the locals as 'The Stalingrad'. It earned this name due to the excessive fighting on Saturday nights, fighting that reminded the locals of the battle then raging between the Germans and Russians over the city of the same name.

One Saturday night the very distressed barman was trying to get the customers to leave. It was closing time. In vain he had called, "Time Gentlemen Please," But the patrons were having none of it. They were too busy singing, making speeches and fighting.

At the centre of all the commotion was Billy Murray and his brothers. The Murrays were notorious. Scrappers to a man, they attended every argument they were ever invited to---and others besides. They would fight at a drop of a hat and if no hat was forthcoming they would find one. Fighting ran in their blood. Their Uncle, Malcolm Murray, had some years before headquartered at, "The Bunch of Grapes" a pub on the Beersbridge Road. They said he would have fought with his own shadow. When he got to fighting, the Peelers had to send a jaunting car with six policemen to get him under control. Invariably he would lock his arms around a lamp post and no one could break his grip. The Peelers would eventually resort to batoning his fingers to break his relentless grip.

People said the Murrays were never at peace unless they were fighting. And this particular night they had, 'The Stalingrad' in an uproar. In desperation the bar man sent for the Police and Davy Magee was dispatched to clear the pub.

Davy was not actually a real policeman. In his younger days, he had been an undertaker when he had managed the East Belfast branch of Thomas Johnston and Sons. In recent years, however, Davy had joined the Auxiliary Police and was, in a sense, a reserve Peeler.

Davy, knowing his likely reception at the pub, was in no haste to get there. Slowly he strolled through the streets from Mount Pottinger barracks. One man against a mob; why rush into the lion's den?

Eventually, arriving at 'Stalingrad' he made his way in with no great fanfare or triumphal entry. Then they spied him. A hush fell over the place. Had there been a piano player he'd have stopped playing.

Suddenly a big voice boomed out, "Ah look who's here, it's Davy Magee, Ballymacarratt's own utility peeler."

It was one of the Murrays!

"Have a drink Davy … bartender pour this man a drink."

"Oh no, no, never on duty. Not allowed. Regulations."

"Aye you're right Davy, regulations."

Davey surveyed the scene then said, "Long time since I've seen you men, it's been a few years. Let's see how long would it be," and then lowering his voice and taking on a look of great and earnest pathos said,

"I think the last time I saw you was at your mother's funeral. I buried her."

"Aye you did Davy."

"She was a quare good woman that mother of yours."

"Aye, she was indeed Davy."

There was a long, pregnant pause.

"Everybody loved her."

"Aye they did Davy, everybody loved her."

Another pause.

And she wasn't just good till her own, she was good till everybody."

"Aye she was Davy. That's the God's truth Davy, she was good till everybody."

Mind you she reared you fellows right."

"Aye that's right Davy, you can say that again Davy."

"I don't believe she ever drank a drop in her life."

"You're right there Davy, she never lipped it Davy, never lipped it."

"Mind you she'd be quare vexed if she could see you tonight and the state you're in."

"Deed aye you're right Davy, she'd be vexed Davy."

By this time the tears were starting to trip them. Thoughts of their dear departed mother had calmed their troubled breasts.

"Ach fellas, I think you've had enough for tonight," says Davy.

"Aye you're right Davy. Now everybody, listen up," shouts Billy Murray, "You all need to listen to what Davy Magee says. He's a decent man. Aye and you all need to get to hell home out of this." They obeyed to a man!

And so that was the night Davy Magee emptied Stalingrad without a shot being fired.

Spite and Fight

A wee man, Tommy Cuddy, appeared in court in Magherafelt on charges arising out of an altercation with a neighbour. The neighbour was now pressing assault charges as during the fight he had had a large part of his nose bitten off. The Judge took a dim view of the whole matter and sternly asked the accused, "Did you bite Mr. Johnston's nose off?

"Ach no your Honour, I didn't bite his nose off," protested the wee man; "Sure he bit his own nose off."

My Chances in Court

My Uncle Bill was a Doctor in Coleraine. One of his patients said to him one day, "Doctor Burns, can I ask your advice? "Certainly Hughie, what's on your mind?

"I'm going to court next week and I want to know what you think about my chances. You see I got into a fight with my neighbour and I hit him. Do you think it will go alright for me?"

"You hit him Hughie?"

"Aye I did."

"Then I don't think it will go so well for you."

"Ach, I disagree with you Doctor, I think it will go OK."

"Why's that?" asks my Uncle Bill"

"Because I didn't hit him as hard as I could."

Star Trek

A young man, at the court in Ballymena, was found guilty of robbery and aggravated assault. As the Judge was about to pronounce sentence he paused and looking at the accused said, "Have you anything you would like to say?" The young man reached into his pocket, pulled out a packet of cigarettes, flipped open the top and said "Beam me up Scotty."

When Tommy Connors was arrested the Guard said, "Anything you say will be taken down & used as evidence…" To which Tommy replied, "Please don't hit me again officer…"

Educating The English

Some years ago, in the court in Magherafelt, there was a case of a man from near Tobermore who had owned a ferret. The ferret it seems had escaped into his neighbour's yard and had attacked and killed the neighbour's chickens. He was now being sued for damages and Mr. Evan Burns of Maghera was called upon to defend him.

The solicitor acting on behalf of the plaintiff was a very able courtroom lawyer. His only problem, if problem it be, was he had never thought it important to acquaint himself with the niceties of elocution and thus spoke in a rich, yet broad, South Derry accent.

On the day of the court case there happened to be a visiting English Magistrate presiding over the activities. This poor man was acquainted with neither Ulster speech nor Ulster ways but was soon to receive the beginning of his education.

Not being very sure of the nature of the complaint before him he asked the Plaintiffs solicitor to explain the case.

"Well your Honour d'ye see it's like this" began the solicitor " my client had a lock of wee chickens and banty hens and his neighbour had a wee fart and the wee fart got out and under the hedge and killt my clients hens."

The Magistrate's face greyed, taking on a look of shock. Then peering over his glasses said, "I'm sorry what exactly was it that attacked your client's chickens?"

"A fart your Honour a wee fart."

The English Magistrate was dumbfounded and then with puzzled voice inquired, " And what exactly is that?"

"Ach you know your Honour it's a fart. You know? A fart, it's a wee long fuzzy thing."

In desperation he turned to Mr. Burns asking, "can you shed light on this for me?"

"Yes indeed your Honour, My honourable friend is referring to a ferret."

"That's right your Honour," agreed the Magherafelt solicitor "it was a wee fart."

PRAYER MEETINGS, PREACHERS, PRIESTS AND PRESBYTERIANS

The Sandwich Board

'Great Arter' was a keen and zealous man. On Saturdays he would walk around City Hall in Belfast with Sandwich Boards dangling around his neck. Each week the boards sported a new Bible text that Great Arter had carefully chalked the night before. But zeal, no matter how intense, cannot replace basic spelling skills. Here's how his board read one Saturday………

'THE WICKED SHALL BE TURNED INTO HELL' (Ps.9:17)…. 'YOU HAVE BEEN WARMED'!

The New Convert

Then there was the new convert to the Salvation Army in Bangor who was given the Bass Drum to play at the Open Air meeting. On being asked to give a word of testimony he said, " It's a privilege to be saved tonight, and by the grace of God I'm going to beat the hell out of this big drum".

The Prayer Meeting

During the 1950s a Brother and Sister Kluteck, missionaries to Haiti were guest speakers at a small Pentecostal Church in East Belfast. No one in the wee church had ever so much as heard there was such a place called Haiti. But, all the same, the faithful were very impressed with the great work being carried on by the couple in that far away place.

At the next prayer meeting, Brother Wiley, feeling exercised to intercede for the Haitian workers, stood and prayed

"Oh Lord, we ask Thee to bless Brother and Sister Klux and the dark souls down in Hades."

At another Missionary prayer meeting Brother Wiley prayed this prayer…

"Oh Lord we pray, tonight, for the people in the uninhabited parts of the world."

Another night he suggested he would lead the congregation in a time of silent prayer.

More from the Prayer Meeting

'Digger' Pitts, a man who for years was not unfamiliar with the pursuit of Saturday night intoxication, suddenly turned 'good living' and began attending the church and the weekly prayer meeting. One night he prayed, "Lord, bless my wife, she the one sitting next to me with the red hat. She says she's a Christian, but then Lord you can never believe what a woman says, can you?"

Fire and Brimstone

Wee Sammy from the Gospel Hall was known as a fiery preacher. Week after week he would warn of the terrors of Hell and the horrors of damnation. His listeners eventually wearied of this ever-repeated theme. They had had enough. This prompted some of the leading men to come to him and plead that he would preach on something different.

" Preach something different? What like?" inquired Wee Sammy.

Well why don't you preach on the Love of God for a change. Take John 3:16 for example 'For God so loved the world'

Wee Sammy assured them he'd give it a try and the next Sunday evening stood up and said

"Brothers and sisters tonight, I want to read from a great and splendid text. Turn in your Bibles to John 3:16; and I am reading from the Authorized Version. It says, 'For God so loved the world that he gave his only begotten Son that whosoever believeth on him should not PERISH'.. Now let us pause there for a moment.'

Big Joe's Prayer

Joe Moore, a big, colossus of a man, stood to pray. Here's his prayer.

"Royal Son of David I am so glad to be met here this morning with thy people. It's great to see Jimmy Hillock here in God's House this morning. It's great to see him praising God this morning for, if you listened to some people, they say he's backslid, they say he's going to the pictures. But here he is, clothed and in his right mind, worshiping Great David's Royal Son.

Amen."

The Ocean Going Vessel

This happened in Magherafelt Christian Workers Union Hall...My parents witnessed the event and laughed about it for years.

A very enthusiastic guest preacher was visiting from Belfast. All evening he waxed eloquent on the terrors of Hell and the delights of Heaven.

Near the end of his sermon he said, "Let me tell you tonight friend, a man without Christ is like a great ocean going vessel. There it is sailing the seven seas, so proudly, so stately. Yet there is imminent danger and disaster waiting to happen for, unbeknownst to the captain and crew, the boat has sprung a leak. There is a hole in the bottom of the boat and it's slowly letting water. The people on board think they are safe and secure, but they are not!

Now listen to me friend tonight. Every man and woman here tonight without Christ is just like that boat. You're proud, you're self-assured, you think you are in no danger, but you're just like that boat. At the bottom of your boat there's a leak. A lethal leak! Certain death and disaster await you if you do not come to the Saviour."

"I was once like that leaking boat before I was saved. But I can testify tonight as I stand before you friends that since I got saved, I no longer have a hole in my bottom."

As you can imagine, the meeting erupted with great mirth and merriment. I don't believe, however, that the wee man ever came back to preach in our district again.

The Paint of Jezebel

The Sunday-School superintendent at a small church in East Belfast was annoyed. He was vexed about the lack of standards in the Church. According to him, there were even young women coming to Church with the 'Paint of Jezebel' on their faces.

He protested, "I don't agree with women having paint on. In fact I don't think they should have anything on."

He should have stopped at "I don't think."

Empty Pews And Preaching Prelates

Many years ago, the then Bishop of Derry was famous for being an awfully boring public speaker. He had emptied every church he ever preached in and, as one wit observed, the poor man had had revival in reverse. He came to Maghera to preach and the Church was completely empty. The Rector, 'Humpy' Knox, was terribly embarrassed. However the Bishop had come to town to hold a service and that was that. So they sang the hymns and said the prayers, but still no one arrived.

At that point the Rector gave the meeting over to the Bishop and the Bishop, not to be deterred, ascended the pulpit and preached to the empty pews.

Afterwards the Bishop asked, "Reverend Sir, did you not tell the people their Bishop was coming?"

The rector nervously shuffled from foot to foot and then confessed, "Well actually, my Lord, I didn't."The Bishop glared at the rector for a moment then said, "Well I'm going to find out who did!"

The Load Of Manure

Many years ago, we had a beloved Presbyterian minister in Maghera who was cultivating the Manse garden. One of his flock, a farmer by trade, on hearing of the project, brought in a tractor load of manure to use as fertilizer. The cleric was delighted and thanked his benefactor profusely. "Ach don't mention it yer Riverence" said the farmer "sure you're worth ten loads of manure any day."

The Good Elder

Some years ago, a visiting preacher came to speak at a Presbyterian Church near Templepatrick. During the course of his address he told a marvellous little yarn about, 'The Good Elder'. The story went something like this. "Once upon a time there was a good elder who was running a wee bit late for church. Now being as he was a good elder he didn't want to be late for church, but as he was rushing out the door he realized he had neither washed nor shaved. Since he was a good elder he couldn't go to the meeting unwashed and unshaved so he rushed to the bathroom to clean up. Well, in his haste, while shaving, he accidentally cut his nose off but not to be deterred and not wanting to be late for church, since he was a good elder, he continued shaving. Then, being in such a rush, he accidentally dropped the razor and cut his big toe off. However, because he didn't want to be late for church, being as he was a good elder, he continued shaving. When he finished shaving, in his haste, being a good elder and not wishing to be late for church, he hastily picked up his toe and stuck it on where his nose used to be and then picked up his nose and stuck it on where his toe used to be. And from that day on every time he wanted to blow his nose he had to take his shoe and sock off.'

The sequel is even better than the story.

After the service an earnest, little, grim faced man, one of the local elders, approached the visiting cleric and asked "Minister, do you see that story you told about the good elder?"

"Yes, what about it?" asked the kindly minister.

"Was it true?"

The minister paused half in unbelief and half wanting to laugh then replied, "Oh no of course it wasn't true."

"Well," protested the local elder, "Don't you think you have better things to do than to come down here telling us a pack of lies like that."

Smooth Things

There was once, many years ago, a Rector in Maghera who had had a long, peaceful and trouble-free ministry with his local congregation. Once when asked of the secret of his success he replied, " I speak only onto them smooth things." Here is an example of his preaching,

"You must repent, as it were, and be converted, in a measure, or you'll be damned, to some extent."

Godless Ballymena?

A man, some years ago, wrote to a Christian bookshop in Ballymena inquiring as to whether or not they had a copy of "Seekers after God" by the Rev. Mr. Farrar. The reply came back, "Sir, we are sorry to inform you there are no Seekers After God in Ballymena. Best try Belfast."

Which Bible Version?

A young ten year old under the tutelage of her grandmother was becoming quite knowledgeable in the Bible. Or at least that's what her Grandmother thought until one day the wee girl asked, "Granny, who was the mother of Jesus? The Virgin Mary or the King James Virgin?"

Of course for years people have argued over which Bible version is the best and most accurate. Old Henry Thompson from near Ballymena was asked his opinion on this matter and he said, "I know they have wrote it and they have re-wrote it. They have writ it and have re-writ it, but the last time they wrote it they writ it right."

Henry Taylor And The Heathens

A special collection was being taken for Dominican Missions one Sunday after Mass. Henry Taylor boasted to Paddy Buckley that he hadn't put any money in the box.

"And why not" asks Paddy.

" Because Paddy me boy I don't believe in Missions."

"Well," say Paddy "then you had call to take some money out of the box."

"I think not?' says Henry.

"Oh I think so," says Paddy Buckley, "Sure wasn't the money for the heathen."

Great Arter's Famous Sermon Outline

'Great Arter' fancied himself as a preacher and a bit of a Bible authority. Being a member of a church that allowed pulpit participation by the membership, 'Great Arter' would occasionally get up and bring a "wee word." One particular Wednesday evening Arter stood to his feet announcing he had cracked the code to the Book of Isaiah. "I have three word which if you memorize" he claimed "will unlock this loftiest of all prophecies.

Young men and young students of the Bible tonight, give particular attention to this great truth I am about to teach you."

Well there was a hush that descended on the meeting like the silence of falling snow. It was as if no one was even breathing. All eyes were fixed on 'Arter'.

Then he continued,

"Here are 'Isaiah's Three Words' now please take note. The first of these great words is, 'SO' the second is," then he paused surveying his audience with Gladstonian authority, "the second is 'LO'. And the third and final word is, 'GO'.

Suppressed merriment and muffled mirth spread throughout the hall but 'Great Arter' didn't notice. Then for emphasis he repeated the words as a man who had just discovered the key to life, "SO, LO and GO."

Jimmy Forsythe turned to Brother Magee and said, "So, Lo and Go? My God! Chinese triplets!"

Mind you, as I've said before, a good laugh can be had from preaching. I should know as I've made many of my own bloopers. But I have to admit I never did preach the following outline that some poor soul came up with when he preached on Jonah.

1 The Iniquitous People

2 The Ubiquitous Potentate

3 The Pernickity Prophet

Cures From A Curate

Wee Annie Murphy kept house for Father Doyle in rural Wexford. One day she came in complaining about her toothache. "It's very bad Father," she said "and no amount of aspirin seems to take away the pain."

"I've got a remedy for toothache which works every time," says Father Doyle.

"Oh, what is it?"

"Well just take your fill of your mouth of water, sit up on the Aga Cooker keeping the water in your mouth, and by the time the water in your mouth comes to the boil, you won't notice the toothache."

Paddy Buckley's Prayer

"Holy Mary, Mother of God, make me a better man and if you can't, don't worry about it for I'm having a really good time the way I am."

The Visiting Minister

The Maghera Presbyterians were to have a guest minister arrive to preach a series of meetings in the church. Being that he was to arrive at the railway station, Sandy Scott, agreed to meet him from the train. As the passengers disembarked unto the platform Mr. Scott surveyed the people. He was unsure which one was the guest minister. Then he saw him. Are you a Presbyterian minister?" he inquired. "No I'm not," came the reply. "Oh sorry," said Sandy, "it's just that you look like one." Oh well you see, said the man, I've been very ill this week with a gastric disorder and that probably accounts for it.

The Priest And The Pig

When Father Doyle first came as a curate to his parish in rural Wexford he began to call with the people in their homes with the purpose of better getting to know his flock. One day he stopped in with Biddy Kelly and she did the 'dacent' thing and offered him a bowl of tea. (In those days it was very common to drink tea out of a bowl, as teacups had not then gained in popularity).

So there they were sitting in the kitchen when suddenly a big pig jumps up, leaning its front feet on the half-door, and began staring straight at Father Doyle. Biddy leapt to her feet and with a swish of her apron chased the pig. Within minutes, however, the pig was back at the door and staring again at the servant of the church. Again Biddy swished her apron and again the pig disappeared only to materialise a few moments later to continue with his relentless gaze fixed on the priest.

"Ach," says Biddy "Never mind that auld pig Father, you see that's its bowl you're drinking out of.

The Rat that Got Away

Dr. R.L. Marshall, the then Presbyterian minister, was visiting my Grandparent's farm at the Mullagh, near Maghera. There were several workers in the fields and the hay was in stooks dried and ready to make into haystacks. Rats tended to take refuge under these stooks and when the stook was lifted the men, armed with heavy sticks, tried to kill any rats running for cover. Someone gave R.L. a stick, after all why shouldn't he make himself useful. The stook in front of R.L. was lifted and R.L. whose sympathies lay with the rat, made a rather pathetic attempt to hit the escaping, fugitive rodent.

Of course the rat got away. Two auld boys were watching the proceedings and one says to the other, "Did you ever in all your life see such an eejit, and him supposed to be an educated man."

Church Bulletin Bloopers

AM Sermon: Jesus Walking on Water.'

PM Sermon: Searching For Jesus.

"National Conference on Prayer and Fasting June 10th 11th and 12th. Price includes accommodation and meals."

The pastor would appreciate it if the ladies of the congregation would lend him their girdles for the pancake breakfast next Saturday.

Don't let worry kill you off - let the Church help.

The Associate Minister unveiled the church's new campaign slogan last Sunday: 'I Upped My Pledge - Up Yours.'

Weeping And Wailing

W.P. Nicholson, the fiery Ulster revival preacher, was waxing eloquent one night on the terrors of Hell. His message was nearing an end when he declared, "Sinner tonight, I warn you most solemnly that in Hell, there will be weeping and wailing and gnashing of teeth."

One old man on the front row began to giggle and said, "Hee, hee, hee, I have no teeth!"

Nicholson thundered back, "Teeth will be provided."

The Preacher's Granny

At another one of his meetings in Portrush, Nicholson was going on and on about the horrors of Hell. He told the spellbound listeners how his dear old Granny had steadfastly refused to accept Christ as her Saviour and had died and gone straight to Hell. He continued then to tell the congregation about how all Christ rejecters would endure the same fate.

In the congregation sat a nurse who kept looking at her watch. She had to be on duty in Coleraine hospital in just a short time, but Nicholson would not bring the sermon to a conclusion. Although she had to get to Coleraine, she was well aware that when anyone in the past had tried to leave Nicholson's services early, the preacher would lambaste them from the pulpit. But time was evaporating and she had to get to work. So eventually she tried, very quietly, to slip out without being noticed. Alas, it was an exercise in futility and Nicholson spotted her from his high, pulpit perch. "Young woman," he thundered, "you are going to Hell."

"Fair enough," retorted the nurse, "Do you any message for your Granny?"

Cain's Wife

W.P. Nicholson was preaching one day at the Belfast shipyard when a heckler called out, "Who was Cain's wife?"

Quick as a flash Nicholson answered, "I respect all honest inquiry after the truth, but I want to warn you young man, don't risk going to Hell by inquiring too much after other men's wives."

The Profane Parson?

The young ministerial student was only delighted when he discovered his fishing guide in Donegal was the same man who took Dr Marshall, former minister of Maghera Presbyterian church, on his fishing trips.

"Do you know Doctor Marshall then?" asked the guide

"Know him? I should think so. He's one of my professors at Magee College."

"He's a great man and a keen fisherman."

"Indeed and he's a great scholar as well."

"Aye deed so he is. Mind you it's a great pity about his tongue."

"His tongue?"

"Ach aye, he's a wild man for the swearing."

"What! Dr. Marshall swears? That's impossible!"

"Oh but he does indeed. I remember once when we were out fishing and he hooked a big trout and just as we were about to net him didn't that auld fish slip off the hook and get away. So, I says to Dr. Marshall, "that's a damned shame," and he said, "Yes indeed it is." But mind you, come to think of it that was the only time I ever did hear him use bad language.

The Day Or The Hour

Wee Matt was a fiery open-air preacher who preached most Saturday nights at the Bank Square in Maghera. Willie Murphy said to him one night, "Matt, I was listening to you this evening and I heard you make a mistake."

"I don't think so," says Matt.

"Oh indeed you did," says Willie "for you said no man knows the day or the hour they will die."

"Well Willie, no man does know, only God knows."

"Well me Uncle Sean knew."

"Ach Willie, how could he possibly know that?"

"The judge told him."

The Maghera Choir

Many years ago the choir from the Maghera Presbyterian Church entered a singing competition. For their performance piece, they chose to sing from Psalms 40, "I Waited For The Lord My God." Afterwards, the adjudicator stared unbelievingly at them and said, "You're like a crowd of boys who wouldn't wait for anybody."

The Disappearing Minister

Some years ago, the Maghera Presbyterian Church had a guest minister come to speak. As it transpired, the guest preacher was very small and being that the pulpit was large and high, the unfortunate gentleman could not be seen when he stood behind it. It was agreed, therefore, that a makeshift and temporary platform be built behind the pulpit and if the dear man were to stand on it, he at least could be viewed by the congregation. The minister, ascended the pulpit and climbed on top of the temporary structure. His intended text was John 16:16 which reads, "A little while and ye shall not see me, and again a little while, and ye shall see me because I go to the Father." However, when the reverend gentleman began reading his text he got as far as, "A little while and yet shall not see me," when suddenly, the temporary framework behind the pulpit collapsed and down went structure, minister and all. Some people said that no more prophetically, accurate words had ever been spoken in the Maghera pulpit.

Water

"Father Duffy," said the old lady after Mass, "that was a marvellous talk you gave this morning. You'll never know what it meant to me. It was just like water to a drowning man."

Mossy Stafford

Meanwhile in County Wexford, Father Doyle needed some help. The grass at the Presbytery was getting long and the chapel needed some repairs. On top of that, the Gaelic Hall was having a new extension put on. A few volunteers had come forward, but much more help was still needed.

Mossy Stafford, a man known more for strength of back than for intellectual abilities was leaving Mass one Sunday when Father Doyle took him aside and urged him to take more of a part in helping with the work at the church.

"Ah God sure don't I know," says Mossy, "but you see I've eight mouths to feed and the work is coming in handy so I don't have much time left over to give you a hand."

"Yes but Mossy" reminded Father Doyle "Man shall not live by bread alone."

Aye you're right there Father," says Mossy, "sure doesn't he need a bit of 'mate' and some potatoes as well."

Young Robert Wilson

Young Robert Wilson from near Maghera, felt called to the Ministry and was eventually accepted to the Presbyterian Theological College for training. Having a son go on for the 'cloth' was no small honour and Mrs. Wilson, Robert's mother, was justifiably proud.

One day, in the early spring, the local minister the Rev. Dr. Marshall, in the course of his annual visitation of the flock, called with the Wilson's. The best tablecloth was produced along with the fine china and the table was spread with all manner of dainties. You see, it's best foot forward time when the minister calls.

All was going well till the conversation came round to Robert. It was then that Dr. Marshall asked,

"How's Robert getting on at college?"

"Ach," says Mrs. Wilson, "he finds the Greek easy enough and the Hebrew quite simple."

"That's good."

"Aye it is, all right, and the Systematic Theology he finds easy. But it's the preaching he has trouble with."

"Oh is that so?"

"Aye it is indeed. You see he works hard on his sermons and gets a great message prepared, but when he stands up in the pulpit to preach, it just leaves him like a fart."

THE EXILES

Free Money

And then there was young Jimmy Holly and the wife who immigrated to the States to seek fame and fortune. Unused as they were to the American ways, they got immersed in the offer of credit cards. At every turn round, it seemed there was 'free' money available; and not being one to look a gift horse in the mouth Jimmy took full advantage of all the offers. But of course the time came when they had to pay the piper, or in this case Sears Roebuck, Dillards, J.C Pennys and a host of others who were now demanding settlement of accounts.

One Friday evening a loud and urgent knock came to the door of their apartment. Jimmy opened the door and there stood a grim looking man who identified himself as being from a leading department store. He was there to collect the debt.

"Come in, come in," says Jimmy, "and I'll make you a wee cup of tea."

"I don't want a cup of tea."

"Have a glass of Coke then."

"I don't want any Coke."

"How about a biscuit?"

'Mr. Holly I'm here about the money you owe, that's all I want from you, so skip this hospitality crap."

"Ach now mister, do you think that you are the only ones we owe money to? And do you see the way of it is this, we believe in fair play. So every Saturday evening we take out our bills and write the names of our creditors on wee bits of paper and put them in a hat. Then we shake it all around and take one name out. Now then whosever name comes out of the hat that's the people we pay that week."

The collections man was enraged.

"Mr. Holly," he protested, "this is no way to do business and my firm will not tolerate this practice."

Just then Jimmy bursts in and say, "now wait a minute there mate. I'd advise you to keep a civil tongue in your head for if you don't change your attitude, I'll not even put your name in the hat the next time

The Telemarketer

My old friend, Dr. Gordon Magee, had a great sense of humour. He was a Belfast man, but lived the second half of his life in Texas. For the final 14 years of his life, due to failing health, he was house bound, but this did not stop him from retaining his zany sense of fun.

One day a young telemarketer phoned to see if she could sell him a subscription to the local newspaper. Here was their conversation.

"Would you like to buy a subscription to the Daily Record?"

"Yes, but tell me has it any pictures?"

"Oh it's got lots of pictures."

"How many exactly?"

She counted up the pictures on each page and gave him the final tally.

"That's nice. But tell me, do you send explainers with the paper?"

"Explainers? What do you mean?'

"Well you see I can't read so I need you to send me explainers to tell me what the stories are all about."

"No, I don't think we have any explainers, but I'll check and see."

"That's very good of you. But it will be very bad if you don't have them. You see, as I was saying, I can't read.

"Oh, is that so?"

"Yes. And it's a terrible affliction not to be able to read. I can't even get from here to San Antonio for I can't read the road signs and I can't read a map."

"Oh that sounds bad."

Aye, it's not only bad, it's worse for you see I'm discriminated against because I'm a minority."

"Oh, I thought I detected an accent. Where are you from?"

"Yugoslavia"

"Yugoslavia? Oh that's nice."

" It's not that nice, for you see it's no fun being a minority. But more than that, I'm in trouble for I was in jail. In fact I just broke out of Jail and I'm on the run.

"You are?"

"Aye and they're looking for me."

"They are?"

"Yes, but they'll never take me alive for I'm sitting here with a loaded gun. And the bailiffs are coming to lay siege to the house, but I'll shoot the first one who tries."

There was a long silence, then

"Well does that mean you don't want the paper?"

"Oh yes, I still want it."

"That's great! So tell me, how would you like to pay?"

"I can't pay, for I've no money."

"But could you not write a check?"

"Well I suppose I could, but I've got no money in my bank account. Do you suppose that's alright to do that?"

"Oh no, no, no, you can't do that, you must have money in the bank before you write a check."

"Well could you not just send me a subscription out as a free gift seeing as I'm from Yugoslavia?"

"Oh no, I'm terribly sorry we can't do that."

"Well then I'll write you a check."

" Great, I'll send you your first copy today. What's your name?"

"Fibber Magee."

"Philber Magee?"

"No, just plain Fibber Magee."

"That's fine sir, your subscription is in the mail."

"Thanks very much, now don't forget to make inquiries about the explainers.

With A Feather In His Cap

Young P.K. McGurk set out for America in search of fame and fortune. In those days there was no telephone so the McGurks were naturally delighted when after a few months the first letters from New York began to arrive.

"Dear Mother and Father" the first epistle began, "Just after I arrived in Ellis Island, I met a man who told me I could get employment at one of the leading department stores here in the city. Within a few short days, I was able to secure regular employment. Now that's a feather in my cap."

Two weeks later another letter arrived. It read, " Dear Mother and Father, each day I arrive at work early and leave late. The manager says he's not encountered such enthusiasm before. Now that's a feather in my cap."

Two weeks later, "Dear Mother and Father, The manager has given me a pay raise because he says I'm a very reliable worker. Now that's another feather in my cap."

Two weeks passed then "Dear mother and Father, the manager has enrolled me in a night class for business management. Now that's a feather in my cap."

Two weeks later "Dear mother and Father, I've been promoted to section deputy. Now that's another feather in my cap."

Two weeks later "Dear Mother and Father, the owner of the store came to visit and he said I was one of his best workers. Now that's another feather in my cap."

Four weeks later, " Dear Mother and Father, I lost my job and am now penniless. Can you please send me the price of a boat ticket home?" Old Johnny McGurk, the father, looked at his wife and said "Just write back and tell him to take all those feathers, stick them in his arse and fly home."

The Car That Wouldn't Turn Left

Ireland has always produced some larger that life characters. One such man I knew was Murty Kane from Borrisokane, Tipperary. Many years ago, he lived for a season near Maghera. This man had made several fortunes and had drunk them. Money flowed through his hands like water, or in his case, whiskey. He was a 'wild man' in every sort of way, but he was the kind of man who'd have given you the shirt off his back at a moment's notice.

I'd heard about a story involving him and a car that wouldn't turn left and I asked him about it one day.

"Oh that was an auld yoke of an auld thing" says Murty "and I near got into a fierce bit of trouble over it."

"Tell me about it."

Without hesitation Murty launched into the saga re-living the story as if it had only taken place yesterday. His eyes lit as he related detail after detail and it seems in a strange way he was almost transported to the days of his youth.

"It's like this," he said. "To understand this story you got to know that I left school young and after farting around for a while I enlisted in the Irish Army. I stayed in for only two years for there was a right ******* of a Sergeant Major who had it in for me. He made me life a living Hell. He was from Galway or Mayo or somewhere like that and I think he just had it in for me for I was from Tipperary. Anyhow, he was unmerciful and looking back on it, even after all this time, I'd have to say he was outright cruel. Well, when me two years was up I decided to leave and nothing could persuade me to re-enlist. I mind well the day I left the Curragh in Kildare. There was I in me 'civies' and the big brute of a Sergeant Major walks over to me with a big smile and him all warm and friendly and sticking out his hand says to me, 'Best of luck now Murty and may God's speed go with you." I took him by the hand all right, but all I said was, "Ye great big ignorant bugger ye, I'll get even with ye even if it takes me my whole life, I don't know how and I don't know where but I'll get ye back." Then I turned around and left. I left, not only the Curragh that day, but Ireland itself.

Off I went travelling from country to country seeking my fortune. Over the next few years, Lady Luck and I entered into an on again off again kind of relationship and by the time I found myself in

Canada we weren't even on speaking terms. I had made my way to Toronto with my last few bob and had just enough money left for one beer. So there was I sitting at a bar sipping me last pint. As it happened, there was a fella sitting next to me and wouldn't ye know, it turns out he was from Ireland, living in Toronto and doing a bit of teaching. Well we got to talking and telling yarns and after a while he says to me,

'Where are you staying tonight?'

"Nowhere, thank God," says I.

'For God's sake man you can't stay on the streets for you'll die of the cold. You can come home to my place as I've a bit of an auld spare room. It's not much, but you are welcome to it till ye get on your feet.

"Well I took him up on his offer and within a short time he had introduced me to some other members of the Irish community. Before long, when it was discovered that I could sell 'snow to the Eskimos,' I began making decent money. It's a marvellous thing how there's a buyer for anything and everything if you can just know where he's hiding. The lads would find me things to sell that no one else could sell and when I'd sell something and make a few bob I'd go away off howling and drinking for two or three days, then come back broke and start all over again.

Well one day the boys phoned me a told me they had a great deal for me. A real earner! It was a brand new Ford Fairlane 500 V8 and I could get it for $500. 'What's wrong with it' says I 'that thing has got to be worth $2500?'

'There's nothing wrong with it' they insisted 'it's brand new but it was in a wee bit of a wreck and although we've fixed it up to mint condition we can't seem to manage to get it to turn left. It will go forward, reverse and turn right but we'll be buggered if it will turn left. Now Murty, ye can have it for $500 and make what ye want on it.'

"But I was broke so I told them I was in no position to buy it."

"Ach never matter about the up-front money," they said. "Just pay us the $500 when you sell the car."

"Well I don't know what possessed me, but I had an auld mad thought that this could be a load of fun and the laughs might be mighty. So I said I'd do it. Now I was still staying with the teacher, but he lived way across town from the garage where the car was. How would I get the car home? The auld yoke didn't turn left and I had a lot of lefts to make.

Well the first thing I did was to give her a name and told her so, for cars are like cattle and dogs, as they like to be talked too. That's why there are so many breakdowns along the road for people don't take time to talk to their cars and I needed all the help I could get from her, so I christened her Princess Petunia. At first we made a bit of progress, but let me tell you it's no simple assignment to take a car like that, Princess or not, across town. "Princess darling, what am I going to do with you?" I asked, and me scratching me head.

Just then it was like a light coming on in my head when I saw right in front of me a set of tramlines. So here, says I to the Princess, let's go for a ride and so we did. We hopped the lines and let them guide us. Now, the wonderful thing about these tramlines is that they will go straight or gently curve left or right and although it took several hours of manoeuvring, The 'Princess Petunia' and I arrived home safely courtesy of the tramline. I'd have thrown a party for the occasion, but as you know I was still broke. But how to sell the car? Think quick! Then I remembered I knew one of the lads from the newspaper and I knew he'd front me the price of an ad. So the next thing the ad appeared in the paper,

1966 Fairlane Ford…..list $2500.

Immaculate. Brand New.

Owner returning to Ireland (due to family emergency).

Must sell quickly. First come first serve at $1500.

Address below. Cash only."

"The next morning, the crowd waiting in line was amazing. They were all pressing and pushing at the front door. So I goes down to them and said are you here about the car, well if ye are you'll just have tay wait yer turn. Who was first, now come on now, who was first?"

" I was," said an old man with the snow of years on his head. Come in then, says I, and we'll talk." As it turned out he was from County Clare…a big mountainey farmer with fists on him like sledgehammers.

"Why do you have to go home to Ireland son?" asked the old man with a hint of concern in his voice, "are there problems?"

"Yes," says I, "Me Da has just died and I need to go home and run the farm for ye see me aged poor old mother isn't fit. She's poorly with the heart, and sits every day in the corner by the fire mourning the loss of me Da. They were married 52 years last week. She's devastated, sure ye know yerself. I have to go home for me Mother and for also I don't want to see the family farm going to wreck and ruin. Now if that thing, with me Da hadn't happened, I'd be staying and keeping that beauty of a car that's outside, but what use is it to me now? So here, I need fifteen hundred and the first man to give me it gets the beautiful Princess."

"But I'd need a drive in her," says the big Clare farmer.

"You do indeed says I, "but better still I'll take you for a drive in her meself and show you the ropes"

"So down we went and jumped into the car. And isn't it marvellous the way the Canadians laid out their cities in blocks. It's so helpful especially when you want to take a man around the block without having to turn left. It's a very easy thing, just go to the end of the road turn right, then right again then another right one more right and you are back home where you started. Right?

"What did you think?" says I to the Clare man.

"God it was mighty, such a smooth motor to ride in but I'll have to ask the wife."

That's a great idea all right," says I "but I've a line of buyers who are dying to get it and the first one of them that offers me $1500 I'll take it. And who knows, at money like this, they'll probably offer me more.

"I'll take it, I'll take it," roared the Clare Man, "I love this car and I love the price."

"Do you have the money on you?"

"I do." And with that he began counting out crisp new Hundred dollar bills and laying them on the dashboard. So, I rolled down the window, stuck me head out and told all the lads who were waiting for a chance to buy that the car was sold, so they'd best be off home now. Well I took the $1500 from the big 'munchie' and gave him the keys of the car. And now if he didn't mind I had my packing to do. Off he went delighted with himself and I went back up to my apartment to change my shirt. It didn't seem as if he'd been gone for two minutes when there was an angry thumping at my apartment door. I opened it and who was standing there but Farmer Clare. I'd seen healthier looking ghosts in my day and before I could say anything, he let the most unnatural curses and swears out of his mouth all intended for me. "What ails ye," says I.

"Ails me? That auld yoak of a motor wouldn't turn left. I tried turning but the car kept on going and in my panic I accidentally hit the accelerator and the car sped on and crashed through a barrier and dropped into a private car park which was down below.

"So where's the car now?"

"It's sitting on top of the roof of a Cadillac, what am I to do?

"Well" says I "I think you ought to do your best to get that auld motor off that Cadillac or the owner of the Cadillac's not going to be too well pleased with you. And with that I ushered him out the door.

The first thing I did was to rush across town and pay me debts. I still had a large charge of money left so I went on the tear for three or four days. But the money, as all money will do, ran out so I came back to the flat. But when I walked in, there was a great gorilla of a young man sitting on the couch. If ye'd have seen him in the movies you'd have thought they were pulling your leg. He was like an angry heavyweight champion on mean and ugly pills.

"Are you Murty Kane?" says he. There was a real menace in his voice. His eyes were chillingly cold and cruel, so I said "No, indeed not, Murty's me roommate. And what did you want him for?" says I.

"He sold me Da an auld car that wouldn't even turn left and it near gave him a heart disorder when he landed on top of a Cadillac"

"How did you get in here " says I?

"The caretaker let me in. I've me own ways of persuasion."

"Well I'll tell you what," says I "Murty will not be back till this afternoon, he's a schoolteacher, so why don't you come back then."

"Be God I'll not, I'm here now and here I'll stay."

"Well fair enough then," says I "but I'm running late for work and I needs to get out of here right quick. I only dropped by to freshen up. So take care now and I hope to see you again and say hello to Murty for me."

"I'll be saying hello with me fists," said the Gorilla, "and don't you think of warning him or I'll come after you too."

Well the big monster waited in the apartment, pounced on my room-mate when he arrived back from school. and gave him an unmerciful hammering. Man a dear he mauled him. He broke bones and the whole works and hospitalized him."

"Did you not feel bad about that seeing as how the teacher had been so kind to you and had helped you out?" I asked

"Ack, in fairness I was sorry for him, but that soon changed for I soon found out who he was."

"Who was he?"

"Well now, remember the bully of a Sergeant Major I had had at the Curragh? You know the one who tormented and bullied me for two years? The one that I said I'd get even with no matter how long it took? And remember I told him I didn't know where or when or how, but I told him I would get him back. Well believe it or not, the School Teacher turned out to be that Sergeant Major's son."

Murty paused, then became philosophical, "You know my friend," says he "I've thought into it and have come to the conclusion that the Bible really is true after all. For the sins of the Father's really are visited unto the children to the third and fourth generation."

Learning to Drive

A lot can be forgotten over the years especially if it was never learned in the first place. This was the case of the returning ex pat arriving in Dublin after twenty-five years in America. Imagine his shock as he got into his rental car at the airport only to find that it was a stick shift (had gears!). He hadn't a clue how to drive it having learned to drive in America in an automatic. However, after a little instruction from the attendant, he carefully set out for the City Centre. All was going well till he encountered his first set of traffic lights. Getting the car stopped wasn't the problem it was getting it going again that was the boyo. There he sat, at the lights, nervously waiting for them to change. Suddenly they were green and off he went, but the car jumped forward and stalled. He had let out the clutch too fast. By the time he got the engine re-started the lights were red again. Looking in the mirror and seeing the ever-expanding line of cars behind him made his nervousness rapidly expand… an unhelpful occurrence for his diminishing driving skills. Then the lights changed, but the car stalled again. He had, in his panic, put the car into third gear. The line of vehicles behind him continued to grow as the lights turn back to red. He's sweating by this stage and when the lights turn green he slowly lets his foot off the clutch and gently pushes the accelerator. Nothing happened. He didn't move an inch. He just sat there like a constipated duck with his engine roaring. By mistake he had accidentally put the car in neutral. Then the light turned red. Just then he looked in the rear view mirror and to his horror he saw a driver getting out of a lorry a few vehicles back. The big burly driver walked up to his window and signalled for him to roll it down. The poor man, in the car, by this stage had gone as white as a sheet. The big lorry driver then sticks his head in the window and with a glint in his eye says, "Excuse me sir, but would there be any particular shade of green you'd be waiting for?"

Out Of The Mouth Of Babes

The Rev Mr. W.P. Nicholson immigrated to the States where he spent many years preaching from City to City. Once when conducting a series of meetings in Los Angeles he stopped a small newspaper boy and asked him the way to the Post Office.

"Go up the street and take your first right."

"You seem like an intelligent young chap," says Nicholson "why don't you come to my tent mission tonight and I will tell you how to get to Heaven."

"Aw go on," said the kid, "sure you don't even know the way to the Post Office."

Gambling, Drink and Tobacco

A young Irish priest, Cahill Collins, who had been studying at a seminary in the States, was assigned, for a summer, to a parish in Kentucky. It was a new church for him and he desperately wanted to make a good impression. On his first Sunday he climbed into the pulpit and preached a scorcher against the 'Evils of Gambling'. He thought he'd done well till several sombre faced gentlemen met him after the Mass and their spokesman said, "Father Collins, we appreciate your sincerity but we think you need to be aware that one third of our income in this Church is derived from people who raise Kentucky racehorses and we feel it would be best to leave the subject of gambling alone."

So the next Sunday young Father Collins got behind the pulpit and preached a blistering message against the 'Evils of strong drink.' Again the same group of men came to him and said, "That was a very thought proving talk and well appreciated, but you need to be aware a third of the income of this Parish is derived from people who make Kentucky Sour Mash Whiskey and it would be best if you also left the subject of alcohol alone."

The next Sunday the young priest got behind the pulpit and let loose against the 'Evils of smoking' and wouldn't you know the same group of concerned men came and informed him that another third of the income of the parish was derived from people who grew tobacco.

For his fourth sermon he preached on, 'The evils of fishing in territorial waters of foreign countries without a valid licence.'

AND A FEW MORE FOR GOOD MEASURE:

The Humpy Backed Man

It used to be common practice in Belfast for the men to jump off the Trams just as they were pulling up to their stop. This practice met with the full approval of the conductors who were always eager to pick up the new passengers and keep things moving. One day a wee man with a humpy back found himself being urged by the conductor to jump off as the Tram was coming to a halt. The wee man was having none of it and said,

"For dear sakes mister, this is a hump I have on my back not a parachute."

I'm Not Myself

Stick leg and Willie Murphy had been drinking for several hours when Stick leg says, "You know Willie, I'm just not myself today." Willie carefully looked him up and down for a minute or two and says, "Who are you then?"

Fishing

Barney Mullan, a Coleraine character, met old Major White and engaged him in conversation. Says Barney, "Have ye been doing any fishing lately Major?"

"Indeed I have my man, I've been fishing near Port Ballintrae there's a great fishing spot there.

"Did you catch anything?"

"Why indeed I did. I caught a huge salmon. It must have weighed twenty pounds."

"Sure I know the place well, I tried fishing there myself."

"How did you get on?"

"I didn't find it that great. In fact my hook got caught on something and I had to swim out to see if I could release it. So I swam out and down under the surface following my line the whole time and eventually found it caught on a sunken Spanish Galleon. What a fine big boat it must have been, for there it sat and the lamps with the candles in them were all still lit."

"Now Barney you don't expect me to believe that do you?

"Well Major it's no harder to believe than the one you told about you catching the twenty pound salmon."

Barney Mullan

One day the Coleraine character, Barney Mullan, was carrying a large old fashioned radio down the town and someone says to him, "that looks very heavy" to which he replies, "Indeed it is not, sure I have it tuned to the light programme."

Another night Barney came home drunk and couldn't get into the house. He eventually got his landlady and she opened the upstairs window and shouted down to him, "You're not getting in." His reply was, "well then throw me down a handful of fleas and I'll make my bed here."

The Brudder

Years ago there were railway lines, and in abundance, all over Ireland. The story is told in Wexford of a young lad, Jimmy Kinsella, being interviewed for a job on the railway.

Thanks to Pat Rafferty for the photo.

The stern Station Master said, " Now young fella, I've got an important question for ye. Let's say you were out one day on the line and you saw a train coming at 60 miles an hour this way and another headed towards it doing 60 and there was only a single track….What would you do?

Young Kinsella thought for a moment then said, " I'd run and fetch me brudder."

"Now why in the name of all that's holy would ye run and fetch your brother?"

"Because me brudder's never seen a train wreck before."

The Battle Of Enniscorthy

Paddy Buckley of near Enniscorthy, County Wexford, then in his early twenties, was aimlessly wandering around some fields one Sunday. All of a sudden he was stopped in his tracks by a great guldering voice that boomed, "What are you doing here young man? You're trespassing!."

Looking up he saw a very red faced older gentleman so Paddy says, "And who exactly are you?"

"Why, I'm Lord Killymuck (name changed to protect the innocent) and I own this land."

"You do? And how did you get it?"

"I inherited it from my father."

"And how did your Father get it?"

He inherited from his father and he from his father and so on, back for generations."

"Yes but how did your people get the land in the first place?"

Lord Killymuck paused, then with a voice swollen with pride replied, "Why, we fought for it."

"Then I'll fight you for it."

Paddy Buckley was never stopped again on his Sunday ramblings.

And Now A Short Poem

"Auld McWhurter's bread

Sticks to your belly like lead

Not a bit of wonder

That you fart like thunder

When you eat McWhurter's Bread."

And Now Another Short Poem

'Cuttins cuttins I love bacon cuttins

Ham and eggs may suit auld hags

And other kinds of gluttons

But when I go down to Gresham Street

And into Mary Huttons

I fling my cap beneath the seat

And roar for bacon cuttins.'

And Yet Another

'There was an old Bard from the Bann

Whose verses were so hard to scan;

His friends told him so,

He replied, 'Yes I know, But I always try to fit as many words into the last line as I possibly can.'

The Prince of Wales And The Big Drum

The Prince of Wales, the one who married Mrs. Simpson, was making a visit to County Down when it was decided to give him a demonstration of the Lambeg drums. The Prince, unaccustomed as he was to the beating of 'Slappers' around Windsor Castle was enthralled and delighted by their sound and asked if he could have a go. Of course the locals were only too delighted to oblige and fitted him up, hanging the big drum around his neck. Unfortunately, the crowd, in their excitement, surged in to see the spectacle so much so that the Prince had no room to even move the beaters. At that point a big burly Orange man, taking charge of the situation, shouted out, "Stand back now, stand back everybody and let Mr. Wales bate his drum."

In Dublin's Fair City

Dublin is a city rife with characters. One morning my wife and I were strolling around a street market near the City centre. It was one of those days when although the sky was clear blue, the wind would have chilled you to the bone. It was a lazy wind. I hadn't known what a lazy wind was till Big Mick from Wexford had said one blustery day, "That's a lazy wind that's blowing."

"And what," says I, "Is a lazy wind?"

Says Mick, "It's a wind that would rather go through you than round you." Well this particular morning the wind in Dublin was lazy and on account of it we were just thinking of leaving the market when I happened to see a gentleman selling boots. Thinking a handy bargain might be picked up I began to browse through his merchandise.

"How's it going Sir" says the street trader, "How's business?"

"Ach" says I "You know yourself, it's just ticking along, I'm just keeping the wolf from the door."

"God Sir! No Sir! Dat's a very bad idea," says he

"What is?" says I.

"Keeping the wolf from the door is a bad idea."

"Why so?' says I.

"Because," smiled the man, "you wants to keep de wolf inside the door."

"And why would I want to do that," says I.

"Because," says he "if tings ever get that bad you can always kill him and ate him."

The Great Caruso visits Wexford

The great opera singer Enrico Caruso, during his holiday in Ireland, once stopped at a farm in County Wexford,. All he had wanted was a glass of water but the family were very hospitable and brought him in a made him a meal. The Farmer's wife was quite intrigued with him and asked, "Now what was it you said your name was?"

"I'm Caruso," the great singer replied.

Instantly the Farmer's wife was transfixed. "What an honour," she said "what an honour to have the famous world traveller Robinson Crusoe stop off in our wee house."

The Accounts Department

The accounts department from a local Wexford Newspaper sent a notice to one Mr. Jimmy Curran stating that his subscription had expired. The note came back with these words written on it, "So's our Jimmy."

You want to see me now!

Paddy Buckley and Jimmy Cooper were drinking one day in Rackard's of Caim, County Wexford. They were both the worse for wear. Jimmy says, "you know Paddy when I was born I was only two pounds weight.

"Did you live?" asks Paddy.

"I did indeed," says Jimmy 'and I grew up to be a big strapping man of six foot four. You want to see me now!"

Vanity, Vanity All Is Vanity

One night Mary Jane Clooney was sitting alone in the corner of Rackard's Pub and Paddy Buckley says to her "What ails ye Mam?"

"Oh God Paddy Buckley," she says "I'm terrible worried about my mortal soul."

"And why so?" asks Paddy.

"Well," says Mary Jane, "I think I might have committed the sin of vanity."

"And what makes you think that?" asks Paddy.

"Well," says Mary, "every morning I gets up and I looks in the mirror and thinks to myself how beautiful I am."

"Never fear Mary me darling," says Paddy, "that's not a sin, it's only a mistake."

Paddy Buckley And The Flies

It was on a hot summer afternoon when Paddy Buckley went into Rackards of Caim, Co. Wexford.

"How are ye Johnny me boy," says Paddy to Johnny Rackard.

"How am I? I'm destroyed with these flies, that's how I am."

"Well Johnny me boy don't let them disturb you for I'm the very man that can get rid of them for you."

"You can?"

"Ack aye, but it will cost you for me services."

"How much?"

"A pint and a wee one."

"It's a deal."

"Fair enough then, set them up."

So Paddy sat down and began enjoying his drink and eventually emptied both glasses. Johnny Rackard had been watching him and when he saw the last mouthful disappear he says, "Now Paddy Buckley, what about these flies?"

"Not a bother," says Paddy, "Just reach them out to me one at a time and I'll kill them for you."

Fighting the Japanese

The good hearted Tommy Minnis, bless him, a man famous not least for talking to his watch, was another character around Maghera. During the 70s he was our self-appointed and self-imagined town security officer. When he wasn't talking to his watch, I used to converse with him and ask him to tell me about his exploits fighting the Japs in World War 2. One particular day he said, "I remember well being out on the ship and I wus standing looking over the side when there it was, coming like that ….. Tsssssssssss….right across the water …. Tsssssssssss ….straight at me.

"What was Tommy?"

"A Japanese bullet, ….. Tssssssssss… coming straight at me."

"What did you do?"

"I ducked."

Driving Lessons

One time Tommy Minnis decided to take driving lessons. A friend took him out and Tommy found himself on the country roads, behind a wheel, for the very first time. All was going well until a sharp bend was approached. Tommy immediately stopped the car, got out and ran round the corner. When he came back he said to his bemused friend, "It's all right, it's not too severe, I think I can take it in second."

The Watch

Tommy Minnis once worked on road construction on the Tobermore Road. One day, he bought a new watch and was so proud of his purchase that, much to the annoyance of his fellow workers, he proceeded to go around telling everyone the time. This annoying practice continued for a number of days, so a plan was hatched. Tommy's workmates decided to put their watches forward by fifteen minutes. The next day, when Tommy started his daily routine of telling them the time they each corrected him. According to them his watch was running slow. The next day they all decided to put their watches back twenty minutes. According to them Tommy's watch was now running fast.

Poor Tommy! To paraphrase Mr. Shakespeare, "Confusion had now made his masterpiece!" He sat there just staring at his failed timepiece, and you probably know where this story is going. After two days of being told his watch was useless at keeping the time, Tommy threw it under a steam roller.

Tommy Minnis was a man much given to directing traffic. Somehow, it seemed to be his blood. Once, after he had passed out in Patterson's pub, an ambulance was called to take him to hospital . When the ambulance started to reverse up the entry to Patterson's, Tommy got up and started directing it in.

And yet another ambulance escapade

There was a band parade in Tobermore and Tommy badly wanted to go, but no one was willing to take him the three mile journey. Not to be deterred, Tommy, collapsed on the Main Street of Maghera. An ambulance was called to transport the stricken victim to hospital in Magherafelt. Tommy was quickly taken on a stretcher onto the ambulance which then took off in great haste, lights flashing and siren blaring, bound for the emergency room. Of course they had to go through Tobermore and as the ambulance drew to a halt at the stop sign at Richardson's corner, Tommy mysteriously revived and as a man possessed of youthful vigour, jumped out of the back of the ambulance. He was just in time for the start of the parade.

The Patriot

Stirred by patriotic fervour, and motivated by a desire to fight for the Empire during the First World War, James Campbell tried to enlist in the Army.

"What age are you?" asks the recruiting sergeant.

"I'm 42 and fit and well," says James.

"I can see that you are fit and well," says the sergeant, "but I'm not allowed to take anyone over the age of thirty eight. Are you absolutely sure of your age? Why don't you have another think about it."

Campbell paused for a moment, scratched his head and thought.

"Well how old are you?" asked the sergeant.

"I was wrong sergeant," says James, "I just got a bit confused. Sure I'm only 38; it's me auld Mother who's 42."

The King Spoke to Me

Tommy Walkinshaw, during his youth, had spent several years in England. It became widely know, in our small community, that when Tommy has been in London, he had met the King of England and the King had spoken to him. Through the years, because of this widely told story, Tommy's stature grew and grew. As he walked up the street from his home just near the old railway bridge people would point him out to strangers and say, "That's Tommy Walkinshaw, he met the King of England and the King spoke to him so he did."

One day a group of the young lads about the town were talking to Tommy and Pin McDonald said, "Tommy, I hear you met the King of England."

"Yes indeed I did, so I did."

"Could you tell us about it?"

"Well no problem, I'd love till tell youse. There I was walking through wan of them big London Parks and here, right in front of me was the King of England walking, along with his entourage, headed straight for me."

"And is it true that he spoke to you Tommy?"

"Aye deed it is, he spoke to me so he did."

"And what did he say Tommy, what did he say?"

"He told me till get out of the way."

The French Exam

Geordie Wareham was a French teacher at the Rainey Endowed School in Magherafelt. On a pre-Christmas examination one of his students gave back the test with these words written on it. "Only God knows the answers to these questions. Merry Christmas."

Geordie gave back the paper with the notation "God gets an A; you get an F! Happy New Year."

The Bank Inspector's Visit to Maghera

(The following is a story told to me by John Marquess)

A bank inspector had to change buses in Maghera, and had half an hour before his connection to Belfast. With time on his hands, decided to pay the local branch a surprise visit. He dandered along the street and into the bank. There were no customers. Then again, this was a country branch, and was probably Maghera Fair Day, the one day in the month when there was not much happening.

However, aside from no customers, there was no teller behind the counter. "Highly irregular" he thought to himself, as he opened the manager's door, to reveal no sign of the manager.

No customers, no teller, and now no Manager. Out of the corner of his eye, through the back window in the Manager's office he could see the garden and an astonishing sight; sitting on deck chairs on the lawn sunning themselves were the manager and the teller!

"Belfast Head Office will hear of this" he said to himself. Then he had a better idea, he'd put the wind up this pair of country bumpkins.

Reaching across the counter to the teller's side he found the alarm button, and give it two good long presses. Riiiiiiiiing, Riiiiiiiing, went the big bell on the wall out on Main Street.

The inspector stood back from the door, expecting the constabulary from the barracks down Hall Street to burst through the door at any moment...

... Two, three minutes passed, then the door opened.

In marched the barman from Walsh's hotel across the street, past him and out to the garden - carrying aloft a tray with two creamy pints of Guinness.

Stevie Mac's Granny

My good friend, Stevie Mac, had just returned to Belfast after several years overseas. One of the first things he did was to go round and see his Granny.

"How are you Granny?" he inquired.

"Deed son I'm not well," she said in her best Belfast accent

"What's wrong Granny?"

"Ack son I'm kind of depressed this weather, I think I might have caught thon auld "Down Syndrome."".

The Air Raid

It had been a quiet evening when all of a sudden the air raid sirens began to blare. It was the 1940's and Belfast was about to receive another un-welcome visit from the German air force. The only safe place would be the air raid shelters, so Tommy and Nellie, an elderly couple, grabbed their coats and headed for the door. Just then Tommy looks back and sees Nellie standing by the sofa excitedly looking under cushions.

"Come on out of that Nellie, come on quick and let's get out of here," roars Tommy.

"But me teeth, me teeth, I'm looking for me teeth," shouts Nellie in a panicked voice.

"For dear sakes," says Tommy, "come on out of that. Thon's bombs they're dropping, not sandwiches."

The Complaining Neighbour

Mrs. Molly Cody was a big fat woman and a neighbour to Paddy Buckley. Although she had a jolly round face, there never seemed to be a day when she didn't 'give out' to Paddy about some thing or other. "Your Pig broke the fence" or "Your cat is digging in my rose garden." It was always something!

One day she was standing at the fence when Paddy's dog walked up to her, looked her up and down and then, nice as you please, bit her on the bum. Well she let out a yelp that would have raised the dead in two parishes and that evening, when Paddy came home, there she was waiting for him to level her newest complaint.

"That auld mangy beast of yours bit me on the arse and it's just as well for you that no blood was drawn."

"No blood was drawn…he didn't draw blood?"

"Aye, lucky for you he didn't."

"Well I think I have call to send for the Vet to take a look at him."

"To look at him? It was him that bit me, not me that bit him."

"Nonetheless the Vet will have to come and fix him up."

"Fix him up?"

"Aye indeed, if what you are saying is right, he will have to have his teeth sharpened!"

Proper Identification

Jim Harney, the famous shoemaker from New Ross, County Wexford, was stopped by the Guards (Irish police) late one summer evening.

" Where are you going."

"Home," says Harney.

"Can you identify yourself?"

Harney reached into his inside pocket and produced a small mirror, looked it up and down, then said, "Yes it's me alright!"

Drying Out!

Kerry Clark decided it was time to dry out. He'd been imbibing for too long. Someone told him of a marvellous clinic in Dublin that excelled in bringing sobriety to the insatiably thirsty. He contacted them, booked himself in to arrive on a Friday evening and engaged Bob Picken the Taxi man to drive him to the big city. Along the way they passed many inviting drinking establishments until, eventually, Kerry spoke up saying that it would probably be a good idea to say a civilised farewell to his soon to be former ways and that they should stop and have a wee one. Well that started it, and from that point on they stopped in nearly every pub and alehouse between there and Dublin. By the time they arrived at the clinic, they were stupefied. Picken was both legless and speechless and Kerry just a little better off, checked the besotted Picken into the clinic. With that, he left, took Picken's Taxi and went on the tear in Dublin for the weekend. On Monday morning, he returned and checked the now sober taxi man out of the clinic and the pair of them went back home.

Supplies for the IRA

This tale was related by the late Archie Agnew to Mr. RE Burns.

Back in the 1950s a group of Maghera men had been down at Croke Park, in Dublin. Among their numbers was Archie Agnew, sometime leader of the Mid Ulster IRA. On passing a hall on the drive home on Sunday evening they observed that there was some kind of event taking place. So, they stopped and went in to discover that a local society was holding a dance. Archie asked to speak to the man in charge. He told the MC that they were beleaguered nationalist from Mid Ulster and could they but speak for their cause to faithful fellow Nationalists and Republicans gathered in the hall. Permission was granted and Archie took to the platform making an impassioned plea for funds with which to buy supplies for the cause and to relieve the plight of the nationalist orphans and widows. A collection was received and the dear folks of that community were found to be most generous. The Maghera men got back into the car and headed up the road only to discover another dance hall where they repeated the previous performance. By this time they were coming down with money so they decided to stop at the next town and spend their gains. According to Archie, they had received so much that they didn't manage to get back to Maghera for several days.

In and Out at McMaster's

Paddy McKenna was inebriated. He'd been imbibing all day, celebrating as though he had won the grand prize in the Irish Sweep Stakes. He hadn't, but why let bad luck get in the way of a good time? The landlady, Mary McMaster, finally said, "Now Paddy, you've had enough, it's time to go home." But Paddy just sat there asking for another drink. Eventually Mary said, "Now Paddy if you won't go home, I'll have to put you out." Paddy didn't budge. With that, Mary went over to him, caught him by the scruff of the neck and marched him out the back door. Five minutes later, Paddy stumbled through the front door and asked for a dink. Mary, bold as you like, once more marched him to the back door depositing him in the back yard. Five minutes later Paddy stumbled through the front door asking for a drink and Mary repeated the performance. This scenario recurred several more times till eventually, as Paddy was being escorted through the back door, he was heard to say with puzzled voice, "For dear sakes missus, do you own every pub in this town?"

Photograph supplied by Pat Rafferty

The Funeral of Hughie Graham

The last remains of Hughie Graham

Were encased in wood today,

And from the family home in Mullinabrone

The corpse was borne away.

Hughie's Widow, Sarah Kate

Wept, (as befitted her to),

And as we passed down the road, Hughie's wee dog

Raised a hullabaloo.

And we followed the hearse through Mullinabrone,

Ballyagan and into the town.

Hugh Dickie was leanin' on his shovel at the grave,

Smokin' and hangin' around.

And as we all shuffled in to the burying ground,

I says to mesel', sez I:

"Its like rain!" and I turned to wee Tam McAleese,

Sez I, "That's a bad looking sky"

Now there was boys was there from every townland

--- And John Jo McCool from the Glen !!! ---

Sez Jim White, "They cut turf beside other for years"

Sez I, "That explains it then!"

And Hugh's cousin Willie was there. --- "They weren't speakin'

for years!", I said to Jo Graham.

"Aye but he marches the nephew's wife's people" sez he,

"He'll be wantin' to keep well in wi' them!"

Now the preacher'd been goin' a good half an hour,

He was raisin' a terrible row.

And after a bit it started to spit

Sez I, "That'll shorten him now!"

But he was only gettin' goin'! He roared and got on!

He sort of got carried away!

And Andy McFetridge leaned over, sez he

"I doubt we'll be here all day!"

And we stood in the cold, near an hour, by my soul,

Exceptin' for wee Willy Brown,

Who'd a cow that was due and the milkin' to do

And the wife to lift in the town.

The preacher was shoutin' about ha'in' to repent,

In time for the Judgement Day,

When wee Willie leaned over and, under his breath,

Sez-he, ("I'm for slippin' away")

The rain had come on by the time he gave o'er,

It was dark by the time we got out

And the most headed home but a few went across

To "Mickey's" for bottles of stout.

Now that's the end of Hughie Graham

And his corpse so gray and solemn,

And we'll hear no more till a year from now,

In the "In Memoriam" column.

By John B. K. Kerr

The Pub Quiz

In was late in the evening and O'Hara's pub was just getting going. Alec, the owner had called for an impromptu pub quiz and one of the questions being asked was, "In what year did William Shakespeare die?" No one had the answer. Just then Willie Murphy walked in so Alec called over to him. "Willie, what year did William Shakespeare die?"

"Die? Die?" said Murphy, "Sure no one told me that he was even sick."

The Big Moon

One night, Rosemary O'Neill looked out her door in the Market Yard in Maghera and said, "C'mere Mammy till u see the big moon...Paddy O'Neill came out too and said, "Aye its alright, but not as big as the wan they have in Aberdeen."

A Great Job

Wee Tommy Stafford had a job on one of the two independent bus companies that serviced Waterford city during the 1940s. His mother was very proud of him and often used to say that her son got to travel miles and miles outside Ireland every day.

Buddha Murphy and the Cell Phone

Back in the day, when cell phones were just coming onto the market, Buddha Murphy's wife bought him this new invention. Buddha, of course was not his birth name. No indeed, when Buddha arrived in the world his parents announced him as Xavier Patrick Nolan Murphy.

But how did he get that name, Buddha? It's like this, growing up in Limerick he got infected, at a young age, with the rugby bug, and indeed, such was his love for and dedication to the sport that he eventually played as a prop forward for one of the local teams. However, although his exertions around the field on Saturday afternoons were an effective way of burning calories, his consumption of copious amounts of post game pints ensured that, through time, his belly became very pronounced. Thus the nickname Buddha.

As mentioned, Buddha's wife bought him a mobile phone. None of his friends had ever seen one before. Mobile phones were just new on the market. Anyway, a few of Buddha's rugby friends arranged to meet on Friday afternoon for a pint or two and, coming up to six o'clock, Buddha's phone rang. It was his wife announcing that his evening meal was ready. When he hung up the phone, he had a puzzled look on his face and turning to his friends asked, "How did she know I was here?"

How Far To Coleraine?

Many years ago in Garvagh, on the way out of town, there was a milestone on the left hand side, that said 'Coleraine 9 Miles'. This was the distance in Irish miles. Then the council came along and put up a milestone on the right hand side of the road that said, 'Coleraine 11 miles'. This was the measurement in English miles. The people of Garvagh were confused. Would it now take them 30 minutes more to walk to Coleraine? Would they now have to leave earlier than usual? Then a young Mr. Johnny Watt came up with a satisfactory solution. He argued that if the folks walked on the left side of the road they get to Coleraine in the same amount of time and there would be no need to leave earlier. And a number of them did just that.

And now, a Garvagh poem

The Courtship of Hugh William McMullan and Suzanne McVeigh

"The red heifer's a-bullin' " said Mrs. McMullan to Hugh, as he supped at his brochan,

"You may take her the day to thon bull of Mc Veigh's, for I think, in me soul it's a good un.

"And see when you're there if you couldn't be fair to Davy and thon Suzanne,

"For I houl ye thon cutty would do you the best, for they say she's lookin' a man"

Now Hugh William McMullan was forty year auld and his mother was seventy one.

His father had died seven years before and his sisters were married and gone,

The two of them lived on their lonesome there, in a throughother tumbledown shanty

With three heifers, a cow and a saddle backed sow and two or three ducks and a banty.

Now she was aye lamentin' and malcontentin' and greetin' at Hugh to get married:

"I'm bad wae the pains this three or four years and I'm damn'd but I'll soon need carried.

"Thon cutty Mc Veigh would do you the best and she'd nurse your auld mother forby ----"

Till she got him that raised that he threw down the spoon and allowed he would give it a try.

So he shaved and got on him and squared himself up and went down to McVeigh's with the heifer.

They soon got her bulled and, when he saw he was dressed, auld Davy showed Hugh where to get her.

The milkin' was done and Suzanne was down reddin' up and washin' the parlour,

When Hugh William stepped forward and set himself down, lit the pipe and then put it till her.

"Suzanne " says he "if a boy like me was to akse ye, ye'd likely marry?"

"Man I would !" says she "For I'm near thirty three and a girl of my age shouldnae tarry".

So they sat and planned and he held her hand and he swore he would love her for ever,

While behind in the byre was the background choir of the bull serenading the heifer.

And so they were wed and when all's done and said, the bull got the best of the bargain,

For Suzanne and Hugh were aye askew and never done fightin' and arguin'.

The Auld mother died and the heifer miscarried and never did well subsequently.

But the Auld bull got his sport, never cost him a thought and he's grazin' the day, quite contently.

By John B.K. Kerr

With Friends Like This

Paddy Connors, a traveller in the Wexford area, called into to see Father Dungan and asked if he would perform his marriage. "Well," says Father Dungan, "that might be difficult for I don't know you. Do you have anyone who could vouch for you." Two days latter Connors comes back to Father Dungan, this time with a friend and said, "Here Father, John Joe will vouch for me." Father Dungan turns to John Joe and says, "Can you vouch for the character of this man?"

"I can Father."

"Was this man ever married?"

"Never, and neither was his Father before him."

Did You Ever Get Married?

Myley Cassidy was another traveller in the Wexford area. When he was dying, the nuns from New Ross took care of him and tried to make him as comfortable as possible. One day, one of the attending nuns said,

"Miley, did you ever get married?"

"No sister, I did not."

"That's a great shame Miley, a great shame."

"Ah but sister, sure you never got married yourself."

"Oh, that's not so Miley, I am married, I am married to Jesus."

"Is that a fact?"

"Yes it is Miley, it's a fact"

"Well all I can say Sister is that you married into a right 'dacent' family."

Paddy's Cap

Paddy Brien died suddenly. Understandably, his wife was both shocked and upset. Nevertheless, funeral arrangements had to be made and a photograph found for the Mass card. However, the family searched high and low around the house, but couldn't find a decent photo of Paddy anywhere. The entire collection of likenesses of the dearly departed were ones where Paddy was wearing his cap, and not only so, the cap was, in each case, pulled over to the side, almost covering his ear. This would never do! Then a neighbour said, "Take it into Kilkenny Town for there's a grand wee man there, a photographer, and he's got all the equipment. He'll be able to take that cap off Paddy's head." So the widow Brien went into Kilkenny and contacted the photographer. To her great relief, the photographer announced that it would be no problem to remove the cap. But says he, "Tell me then, Mrs Brien, what way did he part his hair?"

"Ach," says Mrs. Brien, "sure won't ye see that yourself when you take his cap off."

The Wooden Leg

They say that Harry McMurray lost his leg on the last day of the "Great War." Since that time he had 'lost' six more, all of them wooden. The folks in Maghera knew him as "Stick Leg" but yet others dubbed him "Harry Eight Legs" or "Harry the Eight Legged Wonder." Little giggling children could often be seen walking single filed in his wake imitating his pronounced limp; but Harry didn't seem to mind.

No indeed, Harry didn't seem to mind, partly because the legs had made him somewhat of a celebrity in our small village, but mainly he was unconcerned because, for the most part, Harry spent his days in undisturbed and quiet inebriation.

His brother-in-law was Willie Murphy, and if Harry had a wooden leg, Willie had a hollow one when it came to drink. There was an old saying in our parts about how people drank to forget. This proverb, however, applied to neither Willie nor Harry for there was little that they ever remembered. Their amnesia was due, largely, to the fact that they both shared the same taste in spirits-- methylated spirits --and many a long winter night was spent partaking of the "blow-hard" around a cheerful kitchen fire. Thus they relegated their minds to the regions of perpetual haze discovered by worshippers at the altar of "The Devil's Brew."

It was November. Outside a bitter storm blew with a vengeance.

"That's a lazy wind tonight" said Murphy, "For it would rather go through you than round you."

Being used to Willie and his quips, Harry just sat and smiled as he stared into what was left of the fire. The flames had long ago died and all that remained was a small confederation of glowing coals in the midst of the hearth.

"Willie throw on more coal," says Harry, "for it's no fit night for men or brass monkeys."

"There's no coal left, it's all gone."

"Ach no."

"Ach aye."

" Well the wife had set out some money for till get some more, did we not buy it?"

"Hiv a titter of wit man, sure we spent it all. What do you think we've been drinking all night?"

Harry was silent, but after a moment he rallied and said philosophically, "So we spent it, ---well boys a boys a deary o, I suppose we'll just have to make do ---or maybe we could borrow some from Aggie down the road."

" You can, but I'll not," says Murphy, "I'm not in her good books right now."

"Why not?"

"Well the other night I bumped in till her outside Maggie Peter's and I asked her for the price of a drink. She just stuck up her nose in the air and told me that she had better things to be doing with her hard earned shillings than to buy a drink for an auld drunk like me."

"The cheek aff her!"

"Aye, the cheek aff her, so I called her an auld female dog"

"A what?"

"A bitch Harry, I called her a bitch, aye and worse than that, I told her that if she was in India she's be sacred. Aye and more than that, I told her that she'd never be lonely with a face like that, for with a face like that she could sit home at night and look in the mirror and wonder to herself how she ever got landed with thon, and more too, I told her that she could sue her parents for giving her thon auld face and no court in the land would deny her."

Thus Murphy waxed eloquent while Harry sat in contemplative silence, comforted only in the knowledge that there was drink, and in abundance, to fortify against the wild November night.

Like everything else in Maghera district, morning came at its own pace. Harry was first to stir. He called out, "Willie are you asleep or what? Would you do the dacent thing and pass me my leg?"

Murphy was slumped in sodden slumber in the armchair. His hair was ruffled and there was a small stain on his collar. One glazed eye shot open and just as suddenly closed again.

"Come on Willie," says Harry, "wake up and reach me the auld leg out of the corner there beside you."

"Ach give me head peace the blurt ye, can't ye see that I'm still asleep."

"Aye right enough, how can you still be sleeping when you're talking to me?"

"Fair enough," says Murphy, "I must be awake then."

Murphy sat up, stretched his arms, yawned and passed wind. "Where did you leave the auld leg?"

"In the corner."

"I think not for she's not there."

"Well it's somewhere then."

Murphy got up and made a thorough search of the kitchen.

"Harry me boy, she's clean disappeared."

"How could it disappear?" snapped Harry, "It couldn't just walk off by itself." Then he paused and scratched his chin and said "By all that is holy, you don't think the Leprechauns came and took it?"

"Ach what would a auld leprechaun want with your wooden leg? Sure they're not short of a bit of firewood"

Firewood!!!! It was as if a thunder bolt had struck. Both men let a sudden gasp as their eyes met. Instantly they looked towards the fire. Neither of them spoke for a moment.

"We didn't did we?"

"I don't know."

"It was cold wasn't it?"

"Aye bitter cold."

"But we couldn't have, Could we?"

"I don't think so but look and see."

In a flash Murphy was poking around the ashes. Then he found it. There it was, the metal connecting piece of Harry's leg….

"Well it was a cold night."

"Aye bitter cold."

"What am I going to do?"

"I don't know ye can either laugh or ye can cry, or we can go down quick and see Mr. Burns."

"Mr. Burns?"

"Aye for he's the man that can fix it."

" Ach Willie, Mr. Burns is a solicitor what can he do, he doesn't sell wooden legs."

"Lord give me patience and give Harry a brain," exclaimed Murphy. "I know he doesn't sell wooden legs, but if any man can fix you up with a new leg its him."

No one in the village paid much attention to the two men and they made their way to Mr. Burns' office. Murphy a little unsteady on his feet kept a watchful eye on Harry who was making the short journey, ably assisted by his crutch.

After waiting for a few moments in the reception area they were admitted to the solicitor's inner sanctum. "Good morning gentlemen," said Mr. Burns, "and how are you today?" Harry didn't seem to hear the greeting but Murphy replied. "If I was doing any better, Mr. Burns I'd be sick"

"And how may I help you gentlemen? enquired the clear minded solicitor who chose not to respond with either sympathy or gladness to Murphy's statement. After all how does one say that one is glad that a person is almost sick or sorry that he's almost well? It was much like the time when the Presbyterian minister's wife announced to him that her husband had died and gone to heaven." If the statement were true, how could he offer his condolence? Could he say, "I'm sorry, my good lady, that your husband is in heaven." That hardly seemed the appropriate response. Thus, through this and many other events, Mr. Burns had learnt to act like the true professional.

"We're not come about a legal matter" said Murphy, "but it is like this, somewhere in the middle of the night someone stole Harry's leg."

"This then would be a matter for Sergeant Murdoch and the police," said Mr. Burns gravely as he peered over his glasses.

Harry sat bolt upright in his chair. The name of Murdoch, the original zero tolerance man, struck fear into the heart of the innocent and guilty alike. "No one stole the leg Mr. Burns," declared Harry, "as best we can work it out we were a bit the worse for wear and being as it was a cold auld night and we had no coal we must have burnt the leg to keep us warm."

" You burnt you leg in lieu of firewood?"

"Aye we did, it was the drink and the cold, och it should never have happened, but, howinever, it did and we were wondering if you could help us, being as how I lost the first leg fighting for the King against the Huns and, if I'd been able, I'd have gone to fight against Mr. Hilter." "That," quipped Murphy, "would have put the fear of God into auld Adolph if he'd heard you'd signed up Harry. They'd have probably sued for peace within a few days."

Harry was just about to add a suitable rejoinder when the solicitor interjected "I take it then that you wish me to apply, on your behalf, to the British Legion, stating that you have met with an accident which accident has rendered your leg both unusable and unsuitable for further service."

" Boys a dear," said Murphy, "I couldn't say it any better if I writ it meself."

"Why thank you Mr. Murphy" responded the lawyer with a tone of civility. "I'll attend to the matter at once."

With that, he rose to his feet and shook their hands and bade them good day.

Mr Burns was as good as his word. Within a few weeks, Harry had taken possession of his new member and had now become the man with nine legs. "Thank God" said he "that I'm not a cat."

"Why's that?" asked Murphy.

"Because," said Harry, with great glee and delight, "I'd be on my last legs."

"I don't get it" said Murphy. "But then I never was any good at geography."

John Joe and the Close Shave

The Flying Barber, (John Joe 'Fairy' Campbell') travelled the country on his bike giving haircuts and shaves to any and all who called for his services. One time he had been asked to stop with Father Duffy. This was all well and good, but unfortunately, the Fairy, although a man of strong teetotalistic principles, was occasionally given to long seasons of even stronger drink. It was during one of these lapses that he arrived at the Presbytery to give the good parish priest a shave and trim. However, within a few moments the Fairy's shaking hand and cut throat had left several cuts on Father Duffy's face. "Stop" said Father Duffy as he stood up and examined his bloody face. "John Joe, John Joe, this drink's a terrible thing! "It is indeed" said the Fairy, "It makes the skin very tender."

Sonny McKenna and the Mouse

Sonny McKenna, a Maghera barber had a customer, Mick Kelly, who came in from the country on a very regular basis to get a shave and a trim. In those day the cost for this was half a crown. However after a good many years Sonny had to put his prices up to 3 shillings and sixpence. Mick arrived on a Saturday and took his seat waiting his turn. As he sat there, he noticed a wee mouse sticking its head round a corner.

"Sonny," says Mick, "You've got a wee mouse over there."

"Deed aye," says Sonny, "I've tried everything to get rid of it but all to no avail"

"Aye indeed," say Mick "They're wild hard till get rid aff." Eventually, Mick's turn came and he sat down on the chair and handed Sonny a half crown.

"It's gone up" says Sonny, "the price has gone up. It's now three and six."

Well Mick hoked around and eventually found another shilling and reluctantly gave it to Sonny.

When the shave and trim were finished Mick stood up, went to the door then turned and said, "Sonny, I know how you can get rid of that mouse."

"How?" asks Sonny.

"Well," says Mick, "just catch a hold of him and put him up in the barbers chair and give him a shave and trim and charge him 3 shillings and six pence and you'll never see him again.

The Haircut

Old Bob Hassan from Dungiven had very little hair. One cold winter day he came into Seamus Doran's barbers shop and said "Seamus, would you be able to give me a haircut even if I kept my coat on?" Says Seamus, "Mr. Hassan,

"I could give you a haircut even if you left your hat on"

SAYINGS, STATEMENTS, INSULTS AND OCCASIONAL GEMS OF WISDOM OVERHEARD IN MAGHERA AND OTHER PLACES

"He was so mean and tight that he'd lift his pillow in the morning to see if he'd lost any sleep."

"There's not enough hair on his chest to make a wig for a boiled egg."

"The potatoes were that big that you only needed nine to make a dozen."

Willie Murphy: "If I was any better I'd be sick."

Willie Murphy: "My luck's so bad that if I won a half a Mermaid in a raffle it would be sure to be the fishy half."

"When a man dies in his sleep he doesn't know a thing about it until he wakes up the next morning."

Stick Leg McMurray: "Brandy is very good for the stomach. It's the auld Cognac that does me in."

"Don't trust him. He's only your friend from the teeth out."

On a gray and overcast day this conversation was overheard,

Stick Leg McMurray: "That's a terrible day."

Willie Murphy: "It is indeed, but I'd like to see you making a better one."

Tommy Joe: "I'm that sick that if I was a Catholic I'd have already been given the last rights."

"He's an unfortunate poor auld crater. Life cast him overboard but, unlike Jonah, he didn't find a big fish."

"He's been broke all his life for he never missed an occasion to waste an opportunity."

George Moore: "I attribute my long and healthy life to the fact that I never touched a cigarette, a drink or a girl until I was ten."

"If I throw a stick will you leave?"

C.S. Lewis: "He that looketh upon a plate of bacon and eggs to lust thereafter hath already committed breakfast in his heart."

Willie Murphy: "I started out with nothing and still have the most of it left."

Willie Murphy: "Sergeant Murdoch is a fine big strapping man. I wonder what he'd be like if he had a personality?"

"If a man speaks in the forest and there's no woman there to hear him is he still necessarily wrong?"

Willie Murphy: "The amount of ignorance John Joe has accumulated in one life time is amazing."

John Joe: "How are your relations? I ask that advisedly for I know you have no friends."

Stick Leg McMurray: "Are you tired Willie?"

Murphy: "I don't know! My body and I aren't on speaking terms."

"Make yourself at home where you ought to be."

Willie Murphy: "The Fairy Campbell didn't look well. In fact I've seen several better looking Mummies."

"The cow should not mourn because she cannot sing and the more ye know the less the better."

"He comes from an illustrious line of bad public speakers in the Mayoral office and has brought it to a new low."

Photo supplied by Kevin Daly

Pat McKenna: "I've been all over Ireland in many places"

Willie Murphy: "For dear sakes Pat, how could you be all over Ireland and even be in one place?"

"There he was, hopping round like an Irishman's flea."

"He was a bad looking man. His face looked like it had been scratched by the fingernails of Hell."

Rat O'Neill: "I'm going away for a week and seven days."

"He's a dog in a manger. He can't eat the hay, but he won't let the cows in to get it."

"He looked like something that fell off a flitting."

"Her hearing is that good she can hear the neighbours change their minds."

"If ignorance was music she'd be a brass band."

"I don't like him. In fact, I think if he was at college he would get an F in ART."

"He's a mouse studying to be a rat."

"I'm a big man, but a wee coat fits me."

"He's often mistaken, but never in doubt."

"If she was in India, she'd be sacred."

I'm not saying his opinion of himself is inflated, but recently I remarked on it being a beautiful day and he replied, "Don't mention it, you're very welcome."

"The four of them headed off for the big dance in Enniscorthy. When I saw them go, I realized there must have been half a ton of premeditated mortal sin in that car."

"He's got a personality disorder. He doesn't think he's worthy to fasten his own shoes."

Stick Leg McMurray: "He wants to come and see you, he says he knows your cousin."

Murphy: "Ach sure the Devil knows my cousin, but I don't want him to come and see me."

"The only fast I ever enjoyed was Belfast."

"It takes a long handled spoon to sup with the Devil."

"He preached about Hell with such delight you'd have thought he was queuing up to stoke the fires."

"The only Irishman who would tell you that you couldn't drink a cup of tea would be a judge pronouncing the death sentence."

"If she had a brain she'd take it out and play with it."

"He's got two brains. One is lost and the other is out looking for it."

Stick Leg: "Look at the rain coming down."

Murphy: "Well thank God, it's not going up."

Are you listening to me for I can't hear you?

"You need to speak slower."

"No! you should listen faster."

"I was so hungry that I could have ate my own cooking."

"The atmosphere was great! I could have got up and recited 'Napoleon's Farewell to His Granny' and still have brought the house down."

"He's a dead loss that boy. He's on the road to no towns and very few villages."

Willie Murphy: "I hate any day that begins with morning."

"He looked just like a wee chow of tobacco."

"He's got a face on him like a well chewed prune."

"That's a grand cup of tea missus. If the Sea of Galilee had been made out of that, I could have walked on it myself."

"He was that sweet, he'd have killed a diabetic."

"How could anyone with only one head be so ugly?"

Stick Leg McMurray: "What are you doing out of your bed in the middle of the day?"

Murphy: "Ach sure I get up at 12 o'clock sharp no matter what time it is."

"Come on luv, we'll have a half wan."

"But John it's only half nine in the morning."

"Oh! That's OK then, we'll have a soft drink----a sherry or beer or something like that."

"He died at forty and was buried at seventy."

Auld Buckley: "That's a great lep he's got in his step. I think he must have got it for Christmas."

"She was a good soul, but you'd never have guessed it."

"She was old enough to have been King Billy's Granny."

"My cat can't bark. Neither can I do everything you want me to."

"Where's the Pastor?"

"He's in bed wrestling with the theology of getting up."

Auld Buckley: "I'm that hungry I could eat the head of a cow cut off near the tail."

Willie Murphy: "I'm descended from the High Kings of Ireland, but my Coat of Arms is out at the elbows."

Great Uncle Robert: "I can ate well enough and I can sleep well enough but when there's any work to be done, there's a kind of a trimmling comes over me."

The Landlady's Lament: "You three are a pair if there ever was one. Last night you came in this morning and if you think you're going to come in tomorrow tonight, well, you'd better look for somewhere else to live if you want to stay here."

Auld Buckley: "God help me mam! The only things I can keep in me stomach are the things I'm eating and drinking."

Willie Murphy: "I hate mornings! In fact I'm the man who put a D before A.M.

"Nobody ever goes there anymore because it's too crowded."

"He's as dull as sheugh water."

"You'll never plough a field by turning it over in your mind."

Overheard in Dublin: "I could never fix that for I'm mechanically stupid."

"Drop the mechanically."

"He tried preaching a series of sermons on Jonah and went on week after week. By the time he was finished we were just sorry that the big fish hadn't eaten Jonah on the first Sunday and got it all over with."

"As one door shuts, another door closes."

"When he took off his shirt he looked just like a wee pint of milk."

Auld Buckley: "All I had in my hand was my fist."

"Deep down he's very shallow."

Willie Murphy: "I was sober enough to know I was drunk."

"The cup of Ireland's misery has been overflowing for centuries and is not yet full."

John McNeill: "They say that money talks but the only thing it's ever said to me is 'Goodbye Johnny.'

An Irish Blessing:

May you one day be as rich as the Tax Man thinks you are."

A drunk on the Twelfth of July: "I'm not going to kiss the Topes Poe."

"It's unlucky to be superstitious."

Stick Leg McMurray: "It's not bad it's worse, Wee Banty's got cancer.

Murphy: "Aye deed. It's a very popular disease nowadays."

"John McNeill: "His remaining two teeth at the front of his mouth stood like lonely sentinels guarding the entrance to Hell."

"If I've told you once, I've told you a million times, don't exaggerate!"

Willie Murphy: "I'd rather sleep late than catch worms."

"I wouldn't believe him even if his tongue was notarized."

"Aye and I wouldn't believe her even if she was reciting The Lord's Prayer."

Auld Buckley: "Every workman needs a pencil behind one of his two left ears."

"If ye hadn't a coat sure ye'd always be wearing it."

"He just grew and grew and didn't know when to stop. If he'd have been in Castledawson and fell over three times he'd have been in Magherafelt."

"There's no saving in dying after your Supper."

"He's so laid back he thinks valium is a stimulant."

The half of the world's drug addicts and if it wasn't for Prozac, I'd be a drug addict myself."

The offspring of their union was fit for display at the Zoo.

Stick Leg: "Poor auld Mickey he's not the sharpest tack in the packet. God help him."

Murphy: "You're right there. He usually thinks in slow notion."

Willie Murphy: "I just thought I wouldn't do anything this morning 'till this afternoon."

"I was out drinking all day last night!"

"Opportunity only knocks once, so that must be the Jehovah Witnesses at the door."

Stick Leg McMurray: "Does he talk to himself when he's alone?

Murphy: "I don't know, I've never been with him when he's alone."

Auld Buckley: "He had a short leg, but he wouldn't have known only the other one was longer."

"There are beaches there that never were set foot on by the hand of man."

Auld Buckley: "Those gooseberries make just as good strawberry jam as blackberries do?"

"Reality is only a crutch for people who can't handle drink."

Bella Murphy, "A drap aff the blow-hard quare par-boils the gub."

"All generalizations are false, including that one."

"He's a man given to mountain top experiences. He was either on top of the mountain or the mountain was on top of him."

"Just the facts please, just the facts! No more shoulda, woulda, coulda."

Luther: "God must have been surprised when he read the Creeds."

"Consistency is the hobgoblin of small minds."

"He thought the 'nots' in the Ten Commandments were put in by printer's error."

"I didn't come out from under a clocking hen."

Great Uncle Robert on the beginning months of World War II: "They'll carry on with this till someone gets hurt."

Young minister on being asked how he was finding things:

"The preaching is all right, but the praying's a bugger."

"The Tax Man, the Vat Man and the Customs Man… ..They're all runts from under the same sow."

"He's one huge lump of solidified stupidity."

"Never put off till tomorrow the things you can possibly put off till the day after tomorrow."

"She looked like Mother Earth about to give birth to a new Planet."

He was the seven last plagues wrapped up in one!

Stick Leg McMurray: "So she's put on weight?"

Murphy: "Aye, she's spread out through all the earth like the Roman Empire."

Question: What's the difference between a duck?

Answer: One of its legs is both the same.

Auld Buckley: "Now men, line up alphabetically by height; then pair off in groups of three and you other fellas line up in a circle over here."

"If the horse hadn't stopped to fart he'd have won the race."

Ad in the local paper:

'Hang our wallpapers. They deserve it.'

Graffiti on a wall of a partly demolished Belfast building after a German air raid:

'Alterations by Messers Goring and Luftwaffe.'

Alex O'Hara: "Willie, do you want me to put anything in that whiskey?"

Murphy: "Yes. More whiskey."

Get three Ulstermen together and you'll get four opinions.

"Are you reading that newspaper you're sitting on?"

"He's the only man I know who can watch 'Sixty Minutes' in half an hour."

"You should have seen the ring he bought her. It had two diamonds, two rubies and a sapphire all missing."

"The weaker sex is the stronger sex because of the weakness of the stronger sex for the weaker sex."

"Dublin is no place for a poor person unless he's got lots of money."

"One thing about him is that he's not two faced for, if he was, he wouldn't be wearing that one."

"Well it just lets you show you their broughtupness."

Rat O'Neill on the Labour Exchange:

"There's confusion twice confounded in this place. It is a stronghold of incompetence."

Letter from a flustered Swatragh man to a government office stifled by bureaucracy—"Is it true that in your office there is a rule forbidding you to look out of the window in the morning for, if you did, that would mean you would have nothing left to do in the afternoon?"

Rat O'Neill: "What comfort I find in that blessed word, 'Mesopotamia'."

Rat O'Neill: "I'm never well except I'm starving."

"He disappeared like a fart in a high wind."

"He's descended from the Kings of Ireland and still descending."

"All I want is sympathy, but the only place I can find it is in the dictionary."

"My corns are lepping so there's going to be rain."

"Some people can stay longer in an hour than others can in a week."

'Status Quo' is Latin for 'The mess we're in.'

"If you died with that look on your face no one would wash it."

"He's not worth the fill of me cap of roasted snow."

"It's hotter than a goat eating a blowtorch."

"Once, by accident, I flushed myself down the toilet and I haven't been seen since."

"If he walked into the River Bann, down the sides, across the bottom and up the other side, he'd come up bone dry and his pockets full of fish."

Fractured Proverbs: "A stitch in time is worth two in the bush."

"Look before your chickens are hatched."

"It's an ill wind that makes a man healthy wealthy and wise."

"Headaches strike twice as many women as do men."

"The new town sewer is nearing completion, but Paddy Dempsey says he's holding his breath till it's officially finished."

"His death leaves a void which will be hard to replace."

How many Maghera Presbyterians does it take to change a light bulb?

"Why would you want to change that light bulb? That's a perfectly good light bulb. My grandfather gave me that light bulb.

There was a County Derry farmer who loved his wife so much…he almost told her.

Overheard in Enniscorthy; "Our education has gone to the dogs! There's childer coming out of schools nowadays that can't even spell C. H. A. N. can."

"Time is what keeps everything from happening at once."

"I never repeat gossip so you'd better listen carefully the first time."

"The first 45 years of my childhood almost killed me."

"Local politics … the bland leading the bland."

"A bore is a man who keeps talking about himself when all you want to do is to be talking about yourself."

"He was a loyal young lad. He could beat his drum and fart the National Anthem all at one time."

"Back away, there's nothing in front of you."

"Smoking kills. If you're killed, you've lost a very important part of your life."

"Follow me up the road and I'll be up after you."

"Give me apathy or give me something else."

Redd the Road Riley: "Thon eejit deserves to be kicked to death by a donkey and I'm just the one to do it."

"I've had a wonderful evening, but this wasn't it."

Stick Leg: "Do you believe in ghosts Willie?"

Willie Murphy: "Not at all, I've seen too many of them to believe in them."

"He would be out of his depth standing in a car park puddle."

"Let's get on our knees and thank God that we are still on our feet."

Paddy Doherty: "I got a job as a post man. It doesn't pay much, but it keeps me from walking the streets."

"He suffers from delusions of adequacy."

Sign in Hurley Curley's window, 'Open Seven Days a Week and at Weekends.'

"He's depriving a village somewhere of an idiot."

"If farting could make you lose weight, he'd be the thinnest man in Ireland!"

Mickey Shoddy: "It's not pollution that's harming our rivers it's the impurities in the water."

"He has very high moral standards which he consistently fails to reach."

"He reached rock bottom and began to dig."

Stick leg: "Who would want to live till they are 98?"

Murphy: "Anyone who is 97."

"Give a man a mask and he'll act himself."

"That woman has a tongue on her that would clip hedges."

"She's got a tongue that long that she can sit in the front room and lick a spoon in the kitchen."

"Her house is that wee that she can sit on the toilet and pay the milkman at the front door."

"Thon man's that bad that when he dies he'll be thrown into the very bottom of the bottomless pit."

John Joe: "Stanley Matthews isn't a genius at football. Strictly speaking a genius is someone like Norman Einstein."

"It takes a long handled spoon to sup with the devil."

Murphy "I was born in the USA"

Bill Kearney: "I never knew that?"

Murphy: "Aye, I was born in the Up Stairs Attic."

Robert Lamont: "By Jimmidy! Y'er no saft Jahnny!"

"If there's a wrong way to do things, he'll be sure to find it."

"God help me to take things more seriously, especially parties and dancing."

W.P. Nicholson: "The people in our churches are so cold that if you brought a bucket of milk in through the door it would be ice cream by the time it reached the pulpit."

"I've known this man personally since the first day I met him and even before!"

Traditionally, most of Ireland's imports come from overseas."

What ever you say, say nathing!

Whatever you say, say nathing and keep repeating it.

She'd a face on her that would have stopped a clock!

He's a face on him that only a mother could love.

Wexford Tommy: "Are deese eggs boilt, flied, yoasted or yaw?"

Willie Grogan: "When it comes till a bad stomach there's nathin' that bates a potato!"

I was so hungry that I could have ate me own cookin'.

If you don't get this letter, just write and let me know.

"He's that tough he could ate nails and spit rust, so he could!"

"I love to get drunk sometimes all the time!"

"Durn it! I forgot to go to the gym yesterday! That's 10 years in a row now."

"Well it's not often you are right, but you're wrong again."

To err is human: to arr is pirate.

If he was any more laid back he'd be lying down.

Finally, Murphy was famous for paraprosdokians.. (paraprosdokians are figures of speech in which the latter part of a sentence or phrase is surprising or unexpected in a way that causes the reader or listener to reframe or reinterpret an earlier part.) Here are a few commonly used paraprosdokians that Murphy used or wised he had.

"Where there's a will, I want to be in it."

"The last thing I want to do is hurt you. But it's still on my list."

"If I agreed with you, we'd both be wrong."

Knowledge is knowing a tomato is a fruit. Wisdom is not putting it in a fruit salad."

"In filling out an application where it says 'In case of emergency, notify' I put 'DOCTOR'."

"Women will never be equal to men until they can walk down the street with a bald head and a beer gut, and still think they are sexy."

"To be sure of hitting the target, shoot first and call whatever you hit the target."

"You're never too old to learn something stupid."

"I'm supposed to respect my elders, but it's getting harder and harder for me to find one now."

The End

Miles McKee was born and raised in Maghera, Co. Derry/Londonderry. Although he hasn't lived there in many years he is a Maghera man through and through. These yarns have been collected through the years and have been put together at last in this little book. We hope you enjoy it.

Miles can be contacted at miles@milesmckee.com

Made in the USA
Charleston, SC
24 September 2013